Making Words Third Grade

70 Hands-On Lessons for Teaching Prefixes, Suffixes, and Homophones

Patricia M. Cunningham

Wake Forest University

Dorothy P. Hall

Wake Forest University

PEARSON

Boston • New York • San Francisco
Mexico City • Montreal • Toronto • London • Madrid • Munich • Paris
Hong Kong • Singapore • Tokyo • Cape Town • Sydney

Executive Editor: Aurora Martínez Ramos
Series Editorial Assistant: Kara Kikel
Director of Professional Development: Alison Maloney
Marketing Manager: Danae April
Production Editor: Annette Joseph
Editorial Production Service: Lynda Griffiths
Composition Buyer: Linda Cox
Manufacturing Buyer: Linda Morris
Electronic Composition: Denise Hoffman
Interior Design: Denise Hoffman
Cover Administrator: Kristina Mose-Libon

For related titles and support materials, visit our online catalog at www.ablongman.com.

To obtain permission(s) to use material from this work, please submit a written request to Allyn and Bacon, Permissions Department, 75 Arlington Street, Boston, MA 02116, or fax your request to 617-848-7320.

Between the time website information is gathered and then published, it is not unusual for some sites to have closed. Also, the transcription of URLs can result in typographical errors. The publisher would appreciate notification where these errors occur so that they may be corrected in subsequent editions.

ISBN-10: 0-205-58093-9
ISBN-13: 978-0-205-58093-4

Printed in the United States of America

10 9 8 7 6 5 4 3   11 10

Photos: Dorothy P. Hall.

About the Authors

Pat   *Dottie*

Patricia M. Cunningham

From the day I entered first grade, I knew I wanted to be a first-grade teacher. In 1965, I graduated from the University of Rhode Island and began my teaching career teaching first grade in Key West, Florida. For the next several years, I taught a variety of grades and worked as a curriculum coordinator and special reading teacher in Florida and Indiana. From the very beginning, I worried about the children who struggled in learning to read and so I devised a variety of alternative strategies to teach them to read. In 1974, I received my Ph.D. in Reading Education from the University of Georgia.

I developed the Making Words activity while working with Title I teachers in North Carolina, where I was the Director of Reading for Alamance County Schools. I have been the Director of Elementary Education at Wake Forest University in Winston-Salem, North Carolina, since 1980 and have worked with numerous teachers to develop hands-on, engaging ways to teach phonics and spelling. In 1991, I wrote *Phonics They Use: Words for Reading and Writing*, which is currently available in its fourth edition. Along with Richard Allington, I also wrote *Classrooms that Work* and *Schools that Work*.

Dottie Hall and I have worked together on many projects. In 1989, we began developing the Four Blocks Framework, a comprehensive approach to literacy that is used in many schools in the United States and Canada. Dottie and I have produced many books together, including the first *Making Words* books and the *Month by Month Phonics* books. These *Making Words* for grade levels kindergarten to fifth grade are in response to requests by teachers across the years to have Making Words lessons with a scope and sequence tailored to their various grade levels. We hope you and your students will enjoy these Making Words lessons and we would love to hear your comments and suggestions.

Dorothy P. Hall

I always wanted to teach young children. After graduating from Worcester State College in Massachusetts, I taught first and second grades. Two years later, I moved to North Carolina, where I continued teaching in the primary grades. Many children I worked with in the newly integrated schools struggled in learning to read. Wanting to increase my knowledge, I received my M.Ed. and Ed.D. in Reading from the University of North Carolina at Greensboro. I also worked at Wake Forest University, where I met and began to work with Pat Cunningham.

After three years of teaching at the college level I returned to the public schools and taught third and fourth grades and served as a reading and curriculum coordinator for my school district. At this time Pat Cunningham and I began to collaborate on a number of projects. In 1989, we developed the Four Blocks Framework, a comprehensive approach to literacy in grades 1, 2, and 3, which we called Big Blocks. Later, we expanded the program to include kindergarten, calling it Building Blocks. By 1999, Pat and I had written four *Making Words* books, a series of *Month by Month Phonics* books, and *The Teacher's Guide to Four Blocks*, and I retired from the school system to devote more time to consulting and writing. I also went back to work at Wake Forest University, where I taught courses in reading, children's literature, and language arts instruction for elementary education students.

Today, I am Director of the Four Blocks Center at Wake Forest University and enjoy working with teachers and administrators around the country presenting workshops on Four Blocks, Building Blocks, guided reading strategies, and phonics instruction. I have also written several books with teachers. One request Pat and I have had for a number of years is to revise the *Making Words* by grade level and include a scope and sequence for the phonics instruction taught. Here it is—Enjoy!

Contents

Introduction

Many teachers first discovered Making Words in the first edition of *Phonics They Use*, which was published in 1991. Since then, teachers around the world have used Making Words lessons to help children discover how our spelling system works. Making Words lessons are an example of a type of instruction called guided discovery. In order to truly learn and retain strategies, children must discover them. But many children do not make discoveries about words on their own. In Making Words lessons, children are guided to make those discoveries.

Making Words is a popular activity with both teachers and children. Children love manipulating letters to make words and figuring out the secret word that can be made with all the letters. While children are having fun making words, they are also learning important information about phonics and spelling. As children manipulate the letters to make the words, they learn how small changes, such as changing just one letter or moving the letters around, result in completely new words.

Teaching a Making Words Lesson

Every Making Words lesson has three parts. First, children manipulate the letters to *make* words. This part of the lesson uses a spelling approach to help children learn letter sounds and how to segment words and blend letters. In the second part of the lesson, children *sort* words according to related words and rhyming patterns. We end each lesson by helping children *transfer* what they have learned to reading and spelling new words. Children learn how the related words and rhyming words they sorted help them read and spell lots of other words.

Each Making Words lesson begins with short easy words and moves to longer, more complex words. The last word is always the secret word—a word that can be made with all the letters. As children arrange the letters, a child who has successfully made a word manipulates the pocket-chart letters or overhead transparency letters to make the word. Children who don't have the word made correctly quickly fix their word so that they're ready for the next word. The small changes between most words encourage even those children who have not made a word perfectly to fix it because they soon realize that having the current word correctly spelled increases their chances of spelling the next word correctly. In third grade, each lesson includes 13 to 15 words, including the secret word that can be made with all the letters.

In Part Two of a Making Words lesson, children sort the words into patterns. Many children discover patterns just through making the words in the carefully sequenced order, but some children need more explicit guidance. This guidance happens when all the words have been made and the teacher guides the children to sort them into patterns. In third grade, they sort for two patterns—related words and rhyming words. Many lessons contain homophones—words that sound alike but are spelled differently and have different meanings. The children also sort these and talk about the different meanings of the words.

Many children know letter sounds and patterns but do not apply these to decode an unknown word encountered during reading or to spell a word they need while writing. This is the reason that every Making Words lesson ends with a transfer step. After words are sorted according to related words, children are guided to spell new words based on these related words. When the words are sorted according to rhyme, children use these rhyming words to spell other words. Here is an example of how you might conduct a Making Words lesson and cue the children to the changes and words you want them to make. (This lesson is #30 in *Making Words Third Grade*.)

Beginning the Lesson

The children all have a letter strip with these letters: e o u f l p r w

These same letters are displayed in a pocket chart or on plastic tiles on the over-head. Children turn over the strip and write the capital letters on the back and then tear the letters apart.

The words the children are going to make are written on index cards. These words will be placed in the pocket chart as the words are made and will be used for the Sort and Transfer parts of the lesson.

Part One • Making Words

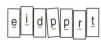

The teacher begins the lesson by telling students what word to make and how many letters each word takes.

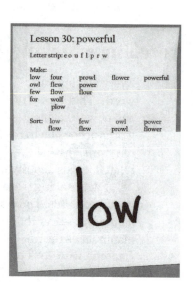

"Use 3 letters to spell the word **low**. We haven't had much rain and the water level in the lake is very **low**."

Find someone with **low** spelled correctly and send that child to spell **low** with the pocket chart or transparency letters.

"Use the same 3 letters to spell **owl**. We saw a white **owl** at the zoo."

"Start over and use 3 letters to spell **few**. We have a **few** new students in our room this month."

"Change the last 2 letters to spell **for**. I brought apples **for** snack time."

"Add 1 letter to **for** to spell the number **four**. I have **four** pets."

"Use 4 letters again to spell **flew**. I **flew** to Florida when I went to Disneyworld."

(Quickly send someone with the correct spelling to make the words with the big letters. Keep the pace brisk. Do not wait until everyone has **flew** spelled with their little letters. It is fine if some children are making **flew** as **flew** is being spelled with the big letters. Choose your struggling readers to go to the pocket chart when easy words are being spelled and your advanced readers when harder words are being made.)

"Change one letter in **flew** to spell **flow**. We watched the water **flow** into the stream."

"Use the same letters in **flow** to spell **wolf**. We were camping and heard a **wolf** howl."

"Use 4 letters to spell **plow**. In the spring, farmers **plow** the fields."

"Use 5 letters to spell **prowl**. Many wild animals **prowl** at night while we sleep."

"Use 5 letters to spell **power**. **Power** is another word for strength."

"Use 5 letters to spell **flour**. We use **flour** to bake bread and cookies."

"Use 6 letters to spell the **flower** that grows in your garden. My favorite **flower** is a daisy."

Introduction

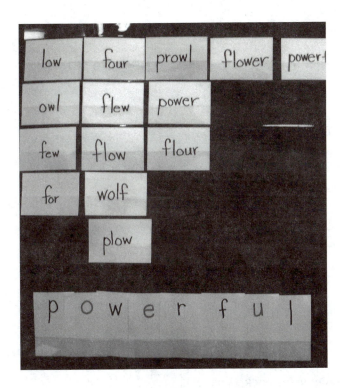

"I have just one word left. It is the secret word you can make with all your letters. See if you can figure it out."

(Give the children one minute to figure out the secret word. Then give clues if needed. "Our secret word today is related to the word **power**.")

Let someone who figures it out go to the big letters and spell the secret word: **powerful.**

Part Two • Sort Words into Patterns

Using the index cards with words you made, place them in the pocket chart as the children pronounce and chorally spell each. Give them a quick reminder of how they made these words:

"First we spelled a 3 letter word, **low**, l-o-w."

"We used the same letters to spell **owl**, o-w-l."

"We used 3 letters to spell **few**, f-e-w."

"We used 3 letters to spell **for**, f-o-r."

"We added the **u** to spell the number **four**, f-o-u-r."

"We used 4 letters to spell **flew**, f-l-e-w."

"We changed the vowel to spell **flow**, f-l-o-w."

"We moved the letters in **flow** to spell **wolf**, w-o-l-f."

"We used 4 letters to spell **plow**, p-l-o-w."

"We used 5 letters to spell **prowl**, p-r-o-w-l."

"We used 5 letters to spell **power**, p-o-w-e-r."

"We used 5 letters to spell the **flour** you bake with, f-l-o-u-r."

"We used six letters to spell the **flower** that grows in the garden, f-l-o-w-e-r."

"Finally, we spelled the secret word with all our letters, **powerful**, p-o-w-e-r-f-u-l."

Sort Homophones

Take one of each set of homophones and line them up in the pocket chart.

for
flower

Have two children come and find the homophones and place them next to the ones you pulled out.

for   **four**
flower   **flour**

Put the words in sentences to show the different meaning, pointing to the correct one as you say each.

"I got a new bike **for** my birthday."

"Two plus two equals **four**."

"The first **flower** just bloomed in my garden."

"**Flour** is used to make pizza dough."

Allow a few children to come and point to a homophone and use it in a sentence.

Sort Related Words

Remind the students that related words are words that share a root word and meaning. Place **power** and **powerful** next to each other in the pocket chart.

power   **powerful**

Use these related words in a sentence to show the meaning.

"When something has a lot of **power** or strength, we say it is **powerful**. Our town was struck by a **powerful** tornado."

Let volunteers tell a sentence using the word **powerful**.

Sort Rhyming Words

Take one of each set of rhymes and place them to form columns in the pocket chart.

low   **few**   **owl**   **power**

Have four children find the rhymes and place them under the words you pulled out.

low   **few**   **owl**   **power**
flow   **flew**   **prowl**   **flower**

Have the students read the rhyming words and confirm that they rhyme and have the same spelling pattern.

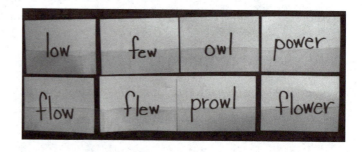

Part Three • Transfer

During the transfer step, we help students use the related and rhyming words to spell other words.

Transfer Related Words

Have students use **power**, **powerful** to spell other words that end in **ful**. Give them help to spell the root word if needed.

> **cheerful**   **thankful**   **painful**

Let volunteers tell a sentence that shows the meaning relationship between **cheer**, **cheerful**; **thank**, **thankful**, and **pain**, **painful**.

Transfer Rhyming Words

Have the students spell these words using the rhyming words to determine the spelling pattern.

> **howl**   **growl**   **tower**   **shower**

Kevin C.

1. cheerful
2. thankful
3. painful
4. howl
5. growl
6. tower
7. shower

We hope this sample lesson has helped you see how a third-grade Making Words lesson works and how Making Words lessons help third-graders learn homophones and how related words and rhyming words help children spell lots of other words.

Spelling and Decoding Skills Taught in Making Words Third-Grade Lessons

Making Words Third Grade contains 70 lessons that teach the homophones, spelling changes, prefixes, and suffixes that third-graders need. In addition to learning to decode and spell words with these prefixes and suffixes, students learn how these prefixes and suffixes change the meanings of words and how these words are used in sentences. Common contractions and compound words are also included in the lessons. All lessons contain rhyming words, which help children review the more complex vowel patterns. Including homophones, prefixes, suffixes, spelling changes, and complex rhyming patterns allows third-graders at all levels to make progress in their spelling and decoding abilities. Making Words Third Grade is truly a multilevel approach in which all students can experience success and learn something new.

Endings, Suffixes, and Spelling Changes

Spelling changes are an important part of the third-grade spelling curriculum. These changes occur when endings and suffixes are added to words. There are many examples for the common spelling changes in Third Grade Making Words, and children who complete these lessons will have many opportunities to discover and practice these changes.

Here are the example words for endings, suffixes, and spelling changes included in the lessons. (The words in bold are secret words.)

s/es   **S** is added to words to make them plural or to make verbs agree with nouns. If the root word ends in **s**, **sh**, **ch**, or **x**, **es** is added to make the word pronounce-able. Normally you can hear when **es** needs to be added after these letters.

ranches	rashes	wishes	boxes
branches	crashes	washes	mailboxes
arches	dishes	radishes	sixes
ashes	rushes	pushes	nixes
cashes	brushes	punishes	

If the root words ends in **y** with no other vowel ahead of it, the **y** changes to an **i** and **es** is added.

cries   dries   tries

ing/ed   **Ing** and **ed** are added to verbs to change how they are used in sentences. If the root word ends in a single consonant and the single consonant follows a single vowel, that consonant is doubled. If the root word ends in an **e**, that **e** is dropped. **Y** changes to **i** and **ed** is added to words that end in **y**.

Examples	Doubling	Drop **e**	**Y** changes to **i**	No change
ing/ed	**shopping**	tiring	cried	trying
	hopping	wiring		**returning**
	subbing	rewiring		turning
	rubbing	writing		rushed
	scrubbing	**rewriting**		brushed
	tipped	used		
	ripped	surprised		
	tripped	disagreed		

er/est   **Er** and **est** add the meaning of "more" and "most" to words. All the spelling changes of consonant doubling, **e** dropping, and **y** changing to **i** apply.

Examples	Doubling	Drop **e**	**Y** changes to **i**	No change
er/est	**maddest**	finest	**funniest**	cooler
	sadder	safer	**unhappier**	coolest
		nicest	happier	**brightest**
		later	drier	tighter
			easier	**stronger**
			runnier	taller
				faster
				nearest
				meanest

er/or   **Er** and **or** are often added to verbs to indicate the person or thing that does the action. Consonants are doubled and **e**'s are dropped when **er** or **or** is added.

Examples	Doubling	Drop **e**	No Change
er	hoppers **shoppers** **planners** **beginners** hitter sitter runner gunner	eraser ranger diver giver baker shaker racer tracer user rater rescuer writer rider ruler trader mover voter	**gardeners** reader sender singer eater heater folder founder owner opener hackers backers ringer **dishwasher** browser buyer
or			**collectors** **instructor** **directors** editor

en   **En** is added to words to change how they are used in sentences. If the root word ends in a single consonant and the single consonant follows a single vowel, that consonant is doubled. If the root word ends in an **e**, that **e** is dropped.

Examples	Doubling	Drop **e**	No Change
en	gotten rotten **forgotten**	ripen given shaken wakens woken broken	olden golden weakens lessen

y   When **y** is added to words, they often become adjectives. If the root word ends in **e**, the **e** is often dropped.

Examples: rusty, crusty, curly, salty, rubbery, scary

al   When **al** is added to words, they often become adjectives.

Examples: **personal, electrical**

ly   **Ly** is commonly added to words to change them into adverbs. If the word ends in **y**, the **y** changes to an **i**.

Examples: really, clearly, **carefully, carelessly**

ful/less The suffixes **ful** and **less** add positive or negative meanings to words.

Examples: **wonderful**, careful, **carefully**, **powerful**, careless, **carelessly**, **thankless**, hatless

ness The suffix **ness** changes adjectives into nouns. **Y** changes to **i** when **ness** is added.

Examples: **weakness**, ripeness, happiness, **unhappiness**

tion/ sion The suffixes **tion** and **sion** are added to verbs to change the verbs to nouns, as in **connect**, **connection** and **discuss**, **discussion**. Sometimes, **tion** and **sion** are not suffixes but just dependable pronunciation chunks at the ends of words, as in **notion** and **pension**.

Examples: action, **vacations**, section, notion, motion, nation, **connections**, election, **exceptions**, **expression**

ture/ sure The suffixes **ture** and **sure** are added to verbs and change the verbs into nouns, as in **create**, **creature** and **please**, **pleasure**. Sometimes, **ture** and **sure** are not suffixes but just dependable pronunciation chunks at the ends of words, as in **picture** and **measure**.

Examples: **creatures**, **departure**, **pleasure**, measure, **measurement**

able/ ible The suffixes **able** and **ible** often add the meaning of "able to " to words. In other words, **able** and **ible** are just dependable pronunciation chunks at the ends of words.

Examples: workable, **unworkable**, **acceptable**, capable, **sensible**, **impossible,** possible

ment **Ment** is commonly added to words and turns those words into nouns.

Examples: **government**, **measurement**, amusement

ous **Ous** is a suffix that turns words into adjectives.

Examples: **dangerous**, **mountainous**

Prefixes

Re, un, dis, and **in/im** are the most common prefixes. Examples are included in these lessons. Spelling changes do not usually occur when prefixes are added.

re When **re** is added to words, it often adds the meaning of "back" or "again."

Examples: reread, reheat, rewire, rewiring, **rewriting**, recall, **returning**, return, rerun, resale, reuse, reseal, remove, reopen, relit, rename

un When **un** is added to words, it often adds the meaning of "not" or changes the word into an opposite.

Examples: unfit, untie, unsent, unripe, **unhappier**, unfold, untold, undo, unsold, **unhappiness**, unpin, unable, unreal

dis **Dis** is another prefix which adds the meaning of "not" or changes the word into an opposite.

Examples: **disagreed**, **discovery**

in/im The prefix **in** (spelled **im** when the root word begins with **m** or **p**) also adds the meaning of "not" or changes the word into an opposite.

Examples: **impossible**, **incomplete**

Homophones

Here are the homophones and the lessons that include them. Third-graders would enjoy making a homophone book, adding pages as they complete the lessons.

Homophone	Lessons Containing Homophones	Homophone	Lessons Containing Homophones
accept except	acceptable (Lesson 46)/ exceptions (Lesson 47)— 2 lessons	pair pear	airplanes (Lesson 24); unhappier (Lesson 20)
ad add	maddest (Lesson 13)	peace piece	appreciate (Lesson 64)
ate eight	paperweight (Lesson 35)	plain plane	airplanes (Lesson 24)
be bee	beginners (Lesson 9); vegetables (Lesson 67); acceptable (Lesson 46), sensible (Lesson 58)	rain rein	airplanes (Lesson 24) ; unhappier (Lesson 20)
bear bare	breakfast (Lesson 25)	rap wrap	paperweight (Lesson 25)
beat beet	vegetables (Lesson 67); acceptable (Lesson 46)	right write	paperweight (Lesson 25)
berry bury	blueberry (Lesson 42)	road rode	rollerblade (Lesson 68); dangerous (Lesson 54)
board bored	rollerblade (Lesson 68)	roll role	collectors (Lesson 10); rollerblade (Lesson 68)
break brake	breakfast (Lesson 25); horseback (Lesson 69)	sail sale	airplanes (Lesson 24); mailboxes (Lesson 51)
by buy	blueberry (Lesson 42)	sea see	vegetables (Lesson 67); weakness (Lesson 61)
close clothes	clothes (Lesson 22)	sell cell	collectors (Lesson 10)
dear deer	gardeners (Lesson 7); disagreed (Lesson 16); departure (Lesson 44)	sent cent scent	connections (Lesson 37); exceptions (Lesson 47)
flour flower	wonderful (Lesson 31); powerful (Lesson 30)	sight site	brightest (Lesson 14)
for four	powerful (Lesson 30)	son sun	instructor (Lesson 11); shouldn't (Lesson 27)
heard herd	dishwasher (Lesson 66)	sore soar	wheelbarrows (Lesson 65); personal (Lesson 56)
here hear	whatever (Lesson 48)	steak stake	breakfast (Lesson 25)
hole whole	wheelbarrows (Lesson 65)	there their	everything (Lesson 23)
in inn	beginners (Lesson 9)	threw through	whether (Lesson 49)/ throughout (Lesson 50)— 2 lessons
knew new	knowledge (Lesson 41); weakness (Lesson 61); unworkable (Lesson 63)	tied tide	tripped (Lesson 2)
know no	knowledge (Lesson 41); unworkable (Lesson 63)	to too two	countdown (Lesson 29)
mail male	mailboxes (Lesson 51)	wait weight	paperweight (Lesson 35)
meat meet	measurement (Lesson 53)	war wore	wheelbarrows (Lesson 65)
one won	wonderful (Lesson 31)	weather whether	whatever (Lesson 48)/ whether (Lesson 49)— 2 lessons
our hour	birdhouses (Lesson 70); throughout (Lesson 50)	we wee	whether (Lesson 49)
pail pale	airplanes (Lesson 24)	week weak	weakness (Lesson 61)
pain pane	airplanes (Lesson 24); unhappier (Lesson 20)	where wear	wheelbarrows (Lesson 65)
		wood would	wouldn't (Lesson 28)/ countdown (Lesson 29)— 2 lessons

Organizing to Teach Making Words

The materials you need to teach a Making Words lesson are quite simple. You need a pocket chart in which to display the word correctly made with the pocket chart letters. You need a set of pocket chart or overhead letters big enough for all the children to see. Also you need index cards on which to write the words children will make and the transfer words. Most teachers store their index cards for each lesson in an envelope.

The children need the letters to manipulate. Reproducible letter strips for each lesson are included at the back of this book.

Making Words Homework

Because children like manipulating the letters and coming up with more words than we have time to make in the lesson, a Making Words Take-Home Sheet is a popular activity. You will find a duplicatable template in the back of this book. Write the letters in the boxes at the top in alphabetical order with vowels and then consonants. Before leaving the classroom, have the children turn the sheet over and write the capital letters on the back.

Making the Homophone Book

To help third-graders remember and keep track of the homophones they have learned from these lessons we are including pages and instructions for a homophone book. Each student can make his or her own book from the templates provided in the back of this book. Each day a homophone is talked about in a lesson, pass out one of the duplicated pages and have your students make a page for their homophone books. This page can be completed by the students in class after the lesson or assigned as homework that day. A few lessons have more than one set of homophones, so the students will have more than one page to do on those days. Some homophones are in more than one lesson; in that case, just have the students make one page for their books the first time. Most homophones have two spellings and two meanings, and so the students will need to write two sentences, one for each meaning, and illustrate the two sentences. Two homophones (*to/too/two* and *sent/cent/scent*) have three spellings and three meanings, and a page is provided for those homophones also. A cover and an index are included for completing each child's book.

If you prefer that your students use a notebook, be sure it has at least 55 pages and use the cover page as a title page, followed by the index page, and then have the students start numbering the homophone pages from 1 to 53. The list is alphabetical but the lessons are done in order in the book, Lesson 1 to Lesson 70. Some lessons will not have a homophone and therefore will not need a page; some will have more than one page for the lesson.

Reference

Cunningham, Patricia M. *Phonics They Use*, 5th ed. Boston: Allyn and Bacon, 2009.

Lesson 1
shopping

Lesson Focus: spelling change: double the **p** when adding **ing**

Letters: | o | i | g | h | n | p | p | s |

 Make Words: in   hip   hop   shop   ship   snip/spin   ping   pong   song
sing/sign   hippo   hopping   shopping

Directions: Tell the children how many letters to use to make each word.

- Emphasize how changing just one letter or rearranging letters makes different words:
   "Add a letter to **hop** to spell **shop**."
   "Change 1 letter in **ping** to spell **pong**."
   "Use the same letters in **sing** to spell **sign**."

- When the children are not just adding or changing one letter, cue them to start over:
   "Start over and use 5 letters to spell **hippo**."

- Give meaning or sentence clues when needed to clarify the word the students are making:
   "Use 3 letters to spell **hip**. My grandma fell and broke her **hip**."

- Give the children one minute to figure out the secret word and then give clues if needed:
   "Our secret word is related to the word **shop**."

 Sort Related Words: hop, hopping; shop, shopping

- Use related words in a sentence that shows relationship. Talk about spelling change.

Sort Rhymes: (with same spelling patterns):

in	hop	hip	ping	song	hopping
spin	shop	ship	sing	pong	shopping
		snip			

Transfer Related Words

- Have students use **hopping** and **stopping** to spell **stepping**, **clapping**, and **shipping**

Transfer Rhyming Patterns

- Have students use rhyming words to spell **strong**, **string**, **chopping**, and **popping**.

Lesson 2
tripped

Lesson Focus: spelling change: double the **p** when adding **ed**
homophones: **tied**, **tide**

Letters: | e | i | d | p | p | r | t |

Make Words: tip rip dip die pie tie tied/tide ride drip trip pride tipped ripped tripped

Directions: Tell the children how many letters to use to make each word.

- Emphasize how changing just one letter or rearranging letters makes different words:

    "Change 1 letter in **tip** to spell **rip**."

    "Add a letter to **tie** to spell the **tied** that you do with shoe laces."

    "Use the same letters in **tied** to spell the **tide** that comes in with the ocean."

- When the children are not just adding or changing one letter, cue them to start over:

    "Start over and use 4 letters to spell **drip**."

- Give meaning or sentence clues when needed to clarify the word the students are making:

    "Use 3 letters to spell **die**. Soon it will be cold and the garden will **die**."

- Give the children one minute to figure out the secret word and then give clues if needed:

    "Our secret word is related to the word **trip**."

Sort Homophones: tied tide
Use a sentence to clarify meaning.

Sort Related Words: rip, ripped; trip, tripped; tip, tipped

- Use related words in a sentence that shows relationship. Talk about spelling change.

Sort Rhymes: (with same spelling patterns):

rip	pie	tide	tipped
tip	tie	ride	ripped
drip	die	pride	tripped
trip			
dip			

Transfer Related Words

- Have students use **tipped**, **ripped**, and **tripped** to spell **stopped**, **clapped**, and **shopped**

Transfer Rhyming Patterns

- Have students use rhyming words to spell **zipped**, **glide**, **bride**, and **gripped**.

12

Lesson 3
scrubbing

Lesson Focus: spelling change: double the **b** when adding **ing**

Letters: | u̲ | i̲ | b̲ | b̲ | c̲ | g̲ | n̲ | r̲ | s̲ |

 Make Words: us bus/sub rub rug snug/sung rung ring sing scrub rubbing subbing scrubbing

Directions: Tell the children how many letters to use to make each word.

- Emphasize how changing just one letter or rearranging letters makes different words:

   "Add a letter to **us** to spell **bus**."

   "Use the same letters in **bus** to spell **sub**."

   "Change 1 letter in **rub** to spell **rug**."

- When the children are not just adding or changing one letter, cue them to start over:

   "Start over and use 5 letters to spell **scrub**."

- Give meaning or sentence clues when needed to clarify the word the students are making:

   "Use 4 letters to spell **rung**. The bell has **rung**."

- Give the children one minute to figure out the secret word and then give clues if needed:

   "Our secret word is related to the word **scrub**."

 Sort Related Words: **sub, subbing; rub, rubbing; scrub, scrubbing**

- Use related words in a sentence that shows relationship. Talk about spelling change.

Sort Rhymes: (with same spelling patterns):

rub	rug	sung	sing	us	subbing
sub	snug	rung	ring	bus	rubbing
scrub					scrubbing

 Transfer Related Words

- Have students use related words to spell **robbing**, **stubbed**, and **grabbed**.

Transfer Rhyming Patterns

- Have students use rhyming words to spell **grub**, **stung**, **cling**, and **shrug**.

Lesson 4
branches

Lesson Focus: spelling change: **es** is added when words end in **ch**

Letters: $\underline{a}$ $\underline{e}$ $\underline{b}$ $\underline{c}$ $\underline{h}$ $\underline{n}$ $\underline{r}$ $\underline{s}$

 Make Words: car care case base arch chase reach beach bench ranch branch search/arches ranches branches

Directions: Tell the children how many letters to use to make each word.

- Emphasize how changing just one letter or rearranging letters makes different words:

    "Add a letter to **car** to spell **care**. Take **care** of your pet."

    "Change 1 letter in **care** to spell **case**. She has a new pencil **case**."

    "Use the same letters in **search** to spell **arches**."

- When the children are not just adding or changing one letter, cue them to start over:

    "Start over and use 5 letters to spell **chase**."

- Give meaning or sentence clues when needed to clarify the word the students are making:

    "Use 4 letters to spell **arch**. The bridge formed an **arch** over the river."

- Give the children one minute to figure out the secret word and then give clues if needed:

    "Our secret word is related to the word **branch**."

 Sort Related Words: **arch, arches; ranch, ranches; branch, branches**

- Use related words in a sentence that shows relationship. Talk about adding **e-s** when words end in **ch**.

Sort Rhymes: (with same spelling patterns):

chase	reach	ranch	ranches
case	beach	branch	branches
base			

 Transfer Related Words

- Have students use related words to spell **reaches**, **searches**, and **benches**.

Transfer Rhyming Patterns

- Have students use rhyming words to spell **vase**, **peach**, **preach**, and **bleach**.

Lesson 5
crashes

Lesson Focus: spelling change: **es** is added when words end in **sh** or **ch**

Letters: | a | e | c | h | r | s | s |

Make Words: has/ash   cash   rash   arch   each   care   scare   beach   ashes   crash
arches   cashes   rashes   crashes

Directions: Tell the children how many letters to use to make each word.

- Emphasize how changing just one letter or rearranging letters makes different words:

 "Use the same letters in **has** to spell **ash**."

 "Add a letter to **ash** to spell **cash**. How much **cash** do you have?"

 "Change 1 letter in **cash** to spell **rash**."

- When the children are not just adding or changing one letter, cue them to start over:

 "Start over and use 4 letters to spell **care**."

- Give meaning or sentence clues when needed to clarify the word the students are making:

 "Use 4 letters to spell **each**. **Each** of us had our own lunch money."

- Give the children one minute to figure out the secret word and then give clues if needed:

 "Our secret word is related to the word **crash**."

Sort Related Words: arch, arches; ash, ashes; rash, rashes;
cash, cashes; crash, crashes

- Use related words in a sentence that shows relationship. Talk about adding **e-s** when words end in **ch** or **sh**.

Sort Rhymes: (with same spelling patterns):

each	care	ash	ashes
reach	scare	rash	rashes
		crash	crashes
		cash	cashes

Transfer Related Words

- Have students use **arches**, **ashes**, **cashes**, **rashes**, and **crashes** to spell **wishes**, **marches**, and **pushes**.

Transfer Rhyming Patterns

- Have students use rhyming words to spell **share**, **beach**, **smash**, and **trash**.

Lesson 6
shoppers

Lesson Focus: suffix **er**, meaning person or thing that does something

spelling change: double the **p** when adding **er**

Letters: | e | o | h | p | p | r | s | s |

 Make Words: pop hop hoe shoe shop rope pope hope hose rose/sore shore hoppers shoppers

Directions: Tell the children how many letters to use to make each word.

- Emphasize how changing just one letter or rearranging letters makes different words:

    "Change 1 letter in **pop** to spell **hop**."

    "Add a letter to **hoe** to spell **shoe**."

    "Use the same letters in **rose** to spell **sore**."

- When the children are not just adding or changing one letter, cue them to start over:

    "Start over and use 4 letters to spell **rope**."

- Give meaning or sentence clues when needed to clarify the word the students are making:

    "Use 7 letters to spell **hoppers**. Rabbits are fast **hoppers**."

- Give the children one minute to figure out the secret word and then give clues if needed:

    "Our secret word is related to the word **shop**."

 Sort Related Words: hop, hoppers; shop, shoppers

- Use related words in a sentence that shows relationship. Talk about spelling change.

Sort Rhymes: (with same spelling patterns):

pop	hose	hope	shore	shoppers
hop	rose	rope	sore	hoppers
shop		pope		

Transfer Related Words

- Have students use related words to spell **shippers**, **trappers**, and **slippers**.

 ## Transfer Rhyming Patterns

- Have students use rhyming words to spell **scope**, **score**, **snore**, and **close**.

Lesson 7

gardeners

Lesson Focus: suffix **er**, meaning person or thing that does something
spelling change: drop final **e** when adding **er**
homophones: **dear**, **deer**

Letters: <u>a</u> <u>e</u> <u>e</u> <u>d</u> <u>g</u> <u>n</u> <u>r</u> <u>r</u> <u>s</u>

 Make Words: end send read/dear deer range erase eraser danger ranger
reader/reread sender garden gardeners

Directions: Tell the children how many letters to use to make each word.

- Emphasize how changing just one letter or rearranging letters makes different words:

  "Add a letter to **end** to spell **send**."

  "Use the same letters in **read** to spell **dear**."

  "Change 1 letter in **dear** to spell the **deer** that is an animal."

- When the children are not just adding or changing one letter, cue them to start over:

  "Start over and use 5 letters to spell **erase**."

- Give meaning or sentence clues when needed to clarify the word the students are making:

  "Use 5 letters to spell **range**. The cows grazed all over the **range**."

- Give the children one minute to figure out the secret word and then give clues if needed:

  "Our secret word is related to the word **garden**."

Sort Homophones: dear, deer

- Use a sentence to clarify meaning.

Sort Related Words: range, ranger; send, sender; erase, eraser;
garden, gardeners; read, reader, reread

- Use related words in a sentence that shows relationship. Talk about spelling change.

Sort Rhymes: (with same spelling patterns):

end	danger
send	ranger

Transfer Related Words

- Have students use related words to spell **teacher**, **farmer**, and **speaker**.

Transfer Rhyming Patterns

- Have students use rhyming words to spell **stranger**, **spend**, **trend**, and **blend**.

Lesson 8
planners

Lesson Focus: suffix **er**, meaning person or thing that does something
spelling change: double the **n** when adding **er**

Letters: <u>a</u> <u>e</u> <u>l</u> <u>n</u> <u>n</u> <u>p</u> <u>r</u> <u>s</u>

 Make Words: ear pan plan lane/lean leap/peal real near/earn Earl pearl learn plane planners

Directions: Tell the children how many letters to use to make each word.

- Emphasize how changing just one letter or rearranging letters makes different words:

  "Add a letter to **pan** to spell **plan**. What is your plan?"

  "Use the same letters in **lane** to spell **lean**. The meat did not have much fat; it was very **lean**."

  "Change 1 letter in **peal** to spell **real**."

- When the children are not just adding or changing one letter, cue them to start over:

  "Start over and use 5 letters to spell **plane**. I will take a plane to see my sister."

- Give meaning or sentence clues when needed to clarify the word the students are making:

  "Use the same letters in **leap** to spell **peal**. We heard the church bells **peal**."

- Give the children one minute to figure out the secret word and then give clues if needed:

  "Our secret word is related to the word **plan**."

 Sort Related Words: plan, **planners**

- Use related words in a sentence that shows relationship. Talk about spelling change.

Sort Rhymes: (with same spelling patterns):

ear	lane	real	Earl	earn	pan
near	plane	peal	pearl	learn	plan

Transfer Related Words

- Have students use related words to spell **winners**, **runners**, and **scanners**.

 ## Transfer Rhyming Patterns

- Have students use rhyming words to spell **crane**, **clear**, **steal**, and **spear**.

Lesson 9
beginners

Lesson Focus: suffix **er**, meaning person or thing that does something
spelling change: double the **n** when adding **er**
homophones: **be**, **bee**; **in**, **inn**

Letters: | e e i b g n n r s |

 Make Words: be in inn see bee big rig ring sing grin green begin singer   beginners

Directions: Tell the children how many letters to use to make each word.

- Emphasize how changing just one letter or rearranging letters makes different words:

  "Add a letter to **in** to spell a different **inn**. An **inn** is a place where travelers can sleep and eat."

  "Change 1 letter in **see** to spell **bee**."

  "Add a letter to **rig** to spell **ring**. She has a new **ring** on her finger."

- When the children are not just adding or changing one letter, cue them to start over:

  "Start over and use 5 letters to spell **begin**."

- Give meaning or sentence clues when needed to clarify the word the students are making:

  "Use 3 letters to spell **rig**. His father drives a **rig**, or big truck, across the country."

- Give the children one minute to figure out the secret word and then give clues if needed:

  "Our secret word is related to the word **begin**."

 Sort Homophones: be, bee; in, inn
Use a sentence to clarify meaning.

Sort Related Words: sing, singer; begin, beginners

- Use related words in a sentence that shows relationship. Talk about spelling change.

Sort Rhymes: (with same spelling patterns):

see	big	ring	in
bee	rig	sing	grin

 Transfer Related Words

- Have students use related words to spell **spinners**, **runners**, and **winners**.

Transfer Rhyming Patterns

- Have students use rhyming words to spell **swing**, **free**, **spree**, and **chin**.

Lesson 10
collectors

Lesson Focus: suffix **or**, meaning person or thing that does something
suffixes **er**, **est**, meaning more and most
homophones: **cell**, **sell**; **role**, **roll**

Letters: | e o o c c l l r s t |

 Make Words: cool tool/loot sell cell role roll toll scoot stroll soccer
cooler coolest collect collectors

Directions: Tell the children how many letters to use to make each word.

- Emphasize how changing just one letter or rearranging letters makes different words:
  "Change 1 letter in **cool** to spell **tool**."
  "Use the same letters in **tool** to spell **loot**. The robbers put their **loot** in a bag."
  "Change 1 letter in **sell** to spell **cell**. I use my **cell** phone every day."

- When the children are not just adding or changing one letter, cue them to start over:
  "Start over and use 4 letters to spell **role**."

- Give meaning or sentence clues when needed to clarify the word the students are making:
  "Use 5 letters to spell **scoot**. Please go quickly; **scoot**!"

- Give the children one minute to figure out the secret word and then give clues if needed:
  "Our secret word is related to the word **collect**."

 Sort Homophones: sell, cell; role, roll

- Use a sentence to clarify meaning.

Sort Related Words: cool, cooler, coolest; collect, collectors

- Use related words in a sentence that shows relationship.

Sort Rhymes: (with same spelling patterns):

cool	loot	toll
tool	scoot	roll
		stroll

 Transfer Related Words

- Have students use related words to spell **sailor**, **visitor**, and **editor**.

Transfer Rhyming Patterns

- Have students use rhyming words to spell **boot**, **troll**, **shoot**, and **pool**.

Lesson 11

instructor

Lesson Focus: suffix **or**, meaning person or thing that does something
suffix **ist** meaning person or thing that does something
homophones: **sun**, **son**

Letters: i o u c n r r s t t

Make Words: run sun son cut nut out our tour sour scour scout counts tourist instruct instructor

Directions: Tell the children how many letters to use to make each word.

- Emphasize how changing just one letter or rearranging letters makes different words:

  "Change 1 letter in **run** to spell **sun**."

  "Add a letter to **our** to spell **tour**. We will take a **tour** of the city."

- When the children are not just adding or changing one letter, cue them to start over:

  "Start over and use 3 letters to spell **cut**."

- Give meaning or sentence clues when needed to clarify the word the students are making:

  "Use 8 letters to spell **instruct**. The builder will **instruct** the workers how to add on the garage."

- Give the children one minute to figure out the secret word and then give clues if needed:

  "Our secret word is related to the word **instruct**."

Sort Homophones: sun, son

- Use a sentence to clarify meaning.

Sort Related Words: tour, tourist; instruct, instructor

- Use related words in a sentence that shows relationship.

Sort Rhymes: (with same spelling patterns):

run	cut	our	out
sun	nut	scour	scout
		sour	

Transfer Related Words

- Have students use related words to spell **artist**, **dentist**, and **inventor**.

Transfer Rhyming Patterns

- Have students use rhyming words to spell **flour**, **trout**, **spout**, and **sprout**.

Lesson 12
directors

Lesson Focus: **or**, meaning person or thing that does something

Letters: e i o c d r r s t

 Make Words: ice rice dice diet/edit riot/trio core score editor credit/direct directors

Directions: Tell the children how many letters to use to make each word.

• Emphasize how changing just one letter or rearranging letters makes different words:

"Add a letter to **ice** to spell **rice**."

"Change 1 letter in **rice** to spell **dice**"

"Use the same letters in **diet** to spell **edit**. I will **edit** your writing with you."

• When the children are not just adding or changing one letter, cue them to start over:

"Start over and use 4 letters to spell **riot**."

• Give meaning or sentence clues when needed to clarify the word the students are making:

"Use 4 letters to spell **diet**. A healthy **diet** is important to both boys and girls."

• Give the children one minute to figure out the secret word and then give clues if needed:

"Our secret word is related to the word **direct**."

 Sort Related Words: **edit, editor; direct, directors**

• Use related words in a sentence that shows relationship.

Sort Rhymes: (with same spelling patterns):

core	**ice**
score	**rice**
	dice

 Transfer Related Words

• Have students use related words to spell **governors**, **inspectors**, and **inventors**.

Transfer Rhyming Patterns

• Have students use rhyming words to spell **twice**, **slice**, and **price**.

Lesson 13
maddest

Lesson Focus: suffix **est**, meaning most
spelling change: double the **d** when adding **est**
homophones: **ad**, **add**

Letters: a e d d m s t

 Make Words: ad add dad sad mad made mate date same tame/team/meat
seat steam maddest

Directions: Tell the children how many letters to use to make each word.

- Emphasize how changing just one letter or rearranging letters makes different words:
    "Add a letter to **ad** to spell the **add** that you do in math."
    "Change 1 letter in **dad** to spell **sad**."
    "Use the same letters in **tame** to spell **team**."

- When the children are not just adding or changing one letter, cue them to start over:
    "Start over and use 4 letters to spell **same**."

- Give meaning or sentence clues when needed to clarify the word the students are making:
    "Use 2 letters to spell **ad**. We found our lost dog by putting an **ad** in the paper."

- Give the children one minute to figure out the secret word and then give clues if needed:
    "Our secret word is related to the word **mad**."

 Sort Homophones: ad, add
Use a sentence to clarify meaning.

Sort Related Words: mad, maddest

- Use related words in a sentence that shows relationship. Talk about spelling change.

Sort Rhymes: (with same spelling patterns):

ad	mate	tame	team	meat
mad	date	same	steam	seat
dad				
sad				

 Transfer Related Words

- Have students use **maddest** to spell **madder**, **sadder**, and **saddest**

Transfer Rhyming Patterns

- Have students use rhyming words to spell **dream**, **flame**, **stream**, and **treat**.

23

Lesson 14
brightest

Lesson Focus: suffixes **er**, **est**, meaning more and most
suffix **er**, meaning person or thing that does something
spelling change: double the **t** when adding **er**
homophones: **site**, **sight**

Letters: | e | i | b | g | h | r | s | t | t |

Make Words: hit sit site hire tire tight sight right bright bitter hitter
sitter tighter brightest

Directions: Tell the children how many letters to use to make each word.

- Emphasize how changing just one letter or rearranging letters makes different words:

    "Add a letter to **sit** to spell **site**, like a construction **site**."

    "Change 1 letter in **tight** to spell the **sight** that means how you see."

    "Add a letter to **right** to spell **bright**. The painting had **bright** colors."

- When the children are not just adding or changing one letter, cue them to start over:

    "Start over and use 7 letters to spell **tighter**."

- Give meaning or sentence clues when needed to clarify the word the students are making:

    "Start over and use 6 letters to spell **bitter**. Some plants have a **bitter** taste."

- Give the children one minute to figure out the secret word and then give clues if needed:

    "Our secret word is related to the word **bright**."

Sort Homophones: site, sight
Use a sentence to clarify meaning.

Sort Related Words: bright, brightest; tight, tighter; hit, hitter; sit, sitter

- Use related words in a sentence that shows relationship. Talk about spelling change.

Sort Rhymes: (with same spelling patterns):

sight	tire	hit	hitter
tight	hire	sit	sitter
right			bitter
bright			

Transfer Related Words

- Have students use related words to spell **lightest**, **kinder**, and **batter**.

Transfer Rhyming Patterns

- Have students use rhyming words to spell **wire**, **slight**, **glitter**, and **critter**.

Lesson 15
stronger

Lesson Focus: suffix **er**, meaning more

Letters:

e	o	g	n	r	r	s	t

Make Words: not nose rose/sore tore torn sort tone stone/notes store snore resort strong stronger

Directions: Tell the children how many letters to use to make each word.

- Emphasize how changing just one letter or rearranging letters makes different words:

    "Change 1 letter in **nose** to spell **rose**."

    "Use the same letters in **rose** to spell **sore**. I have a **sore** foot."

    "Add a letter to **tone** to spell **stone**. I found a white **stone** on the beach."

- When the children are not just adding or changing one letter, cue them to start over:

    "Start over and use 4 letters to spell **sort**."

- Give meaning or sentence clues when needed to clarify the word the students are making:

    "Use 4 letters to spell **tone**. Watch the **tone** of your voice when speaking."

- Give the children one minute to figure out the secret word and then give clues if needed:

    "Our secret word is related to the word **strong**."

Sort Related Words: strong, stronger; tore, torn

- Use related words in a sentence that shows relationship. Talk about spelling change.

Sort Rhymes: (with same spelling patterns):

tore	rose	tone	sort
sore	nose	stone	resort
store			
snore			

Transfer Related Words

- Have students use related words to spell **longer**, **older**, and **taller**.

Transfer Rhyming Patterns

- Have students use rhyming words to spell **score**, **clone**, **phone**, and **throne**.

Lesson 16
disagreed

Lesson Focus: suffix **er**, meaning more
prefix **dis**, meaning opposite
homophones: **dear, deer**

Letters: a e e i d d g r s

 Make Words: sad seed deed deer dear ease edge greed agree grade dredge
sadder easier disagreed

Directions: Tell the children how many letters to use to make each word.

- Emphasize how changing just one letter or rearranging letters makes different words:
  "Change 1 letter in **seed** to spell **deed**. Did you do a good **deed** today?"
  "Change 1 letter in **deed** to spell **deer**."

- When the children are not just adding or changing one letter, cue them to start over:
  "Start over and use 4 letters to spell **ease**. Most of you did that with **ease**."

- Give meaning or sentence clues when needed to clarify the word the students are making:
  "Use 5 letters to spell **greed**. It was **greed** that made the man rob the bank."

- Give the children one minute to figure out the secret word and then give clues if needed:
  "Our secret word means the opposite of **agreed**."

 Sort Homophones: dear, deer

- Give a sentence to make the meaning clear.

Sort Related Words: sad, sadder; ease, easier; agree, disagreed

- Use related words in a sentence that shows relationship.

Sort Rhymes: (with same spelling patterns):

edge	seed
dredge	deed
	greed
	disagreed

 Transfer Related Words

- Have students use related words to spell **madder**, **dislike**, and **displace**.

Transfer Rhyming Patterns

- Have students use rhyming words to spell **wedge**, **ledge**, **hedge**, and **pledge**.

26

Lesson 17
discovery

Lesson Focus: prefix **dis**
suffix **er**, meaning person or thing that does something
spelling change: change the **y** to **i** and add **es** or **ed**
spelling change: drop the **e** when adding **er**

Letters: e   i   o   c   d   r   s   v   y

 Make Words: dry cry very dive diver/drive drove voice video dries cries
cried cover discover discovery

Directions: Tell the children how many letters to use to make each word.

- Emphasize how changing just one letter or rearranging letters makes different words:
    "Add a letter to **dive** to spell **diver**."
    "Use the same letters in **diver** to spell **drive**."
    "Change 1 letter in **drive** to spell **drove**. This morning I **drove** my car to school."

- When the children are not just adding or changing one letter, cue them to start over:
    "Start over and use 4 letters to spell **very**. I have some **very** good students."

- Give meaning or sentence clues when needed to clarify the word the students are making:
    "Use 4 letters to spell **dive**. Do you like to jump or **dive** into deep water?"

- Give the children one minute to figure out the secret word and then give clues if needed:
    "Our secret word is related to the word **cover**."

 Sort Related Words: **cover, discover, discovery; cry, cried, cries; dry, dries;
dive, diver; drive, drove**

- Use related words in a sentence that shows relationship. Talk about spelling change.

Sort Rhymes: (with same spelling patterns):

dry	**dries**	**dive**
cry	**cries**	**drive**

 Transfer Related Words

- Have students use **cries** and **cried** to spell **tries** and **tried**.

Transfer Rhyming Patterns

- Have students use rhyming words to spell **spy**, **spies**, **hive**, and **thrive**.

Lesson 18
security

Lesson Focus: suffix **y**

spelling change: change the **y** to **i** and add **es**

Letters: | u | e | i | c | r | s | t | y |

 Make Words: cry try city cute cure sure rest rust rusty cries tries crest crust crusty security

Directions: Tell the children how many letters to use to make each word.

- Emphasize how changing just one letter or rearranging letters makes different words:

    "Change 1 letter in **cry** to spell **try**."

    "Change 1 letter in **cute** to make **cure**.

    "Add a letter to **rust** to spell **rusty**."

- When the children are not just adding or changing one letter, cue them to start over:

    "Start over and use 4 letters to spell **rest**."

- Give meaning or sentence clues when needed to clarify the word the students are making:

    "Use 5 letters to spell **cries**. The baby **cries** when it is hungry."

- Give the children one minute to figure out the secret word and then give clues if needed:

    "Our secret word is related to the word **secure**."

 Sort Related Words: **cry**, **cries**; **try**, **tries**; **rust**, **rusty**; **crust**, **crusty**

- Use related words in a sentence that shows relationship. Talk about spelling change.

Sort Rhymes: (with same spelling patterns):

rest	cry	cries	cure	rust	rusty	security
crest	try	tries	sure	crust	crusty	city

 Transfer Related Words

- Have students use related words to spell **flies**, **marries**, and **carries**.

Transfer Rhyming Patterns

- Have students use rhyming words to spell **trust**, **trusty**, **quest**, and **chest**.

Lesson 19
funniest

Lesson Focus: suffix **est**, meaning most
spelling change: change **y** to **i** when adding **est**
prefix **un**, meaning opposite

Letters: $\boxed{\underline{e}\ \ \underline{i}\ \ \underline{u}\ \ \underline{f}\ \ \underline{n}\ \ \underline{n}\ \ \underline{s}\ \ \underline{t}}$

 Make Words: fit   tie   fun   sun   stun   nine   fine   nest/sent   unfit   untie
unsent   infest/finest   funniest

Directions: Tell the children how many letters to use to make each word.

- Emphasize how changing just one letter or rearranging letters makes different words:
  "Change 1 letter in **fun** to spell **sun**."
  "Add a letter to **sun** to spell **stun**. The news will **stun** her."
  "Use the same letters in **nest** to spell **sent**."
- When the children are not just adding or changing one letter, cue them to start over:
  "Start over and use 5 letters to spell **unfit**. The soil was **unfit** for growing vegetables."
- Give meaning or sentence clues when needed to clarify the word the students are making:
  "Use 3 letters to spell **tie**."**Tie** your shoes so you won't trip over your laces!"
- Give the children one minute to figure out the secret word and then give clues if needed:
  "Our secret word is related to the word **fun**."

 Sort Related Words: fun, funniest; fine, finest; fit, unfit; tie, untie; sent, unsent

- Use related words in a sentence that shows relationship. Talk about spelling change.

Sort Rhymes: (with same spelling patterns):

fun	fine	nest
sun	nine	infest
stun		finest
		funniest

 Transfer Related Words

- Have students use related words to spell **latest**, **happiest**, and **unhappy**.

Transfer Rhyming Patterns

- Have students use rhyming words to spell **spine**, **chest**, **shine**, and **shrine**.

Lesson 20

unhappier

<table>
<tr><td>Lesson Focus:</td><td>prefix un, meaning not
suffix er, meaning more
suffix en
spelling change: change the y to i when adding er
spelling change: drop the e when adding en
homophones: pear, pair; pane, pain; rein, rain</td></tr>
<tr><td>Letters:</td><td><u>a</u>   <u>e</u>   <u>i</u>   <u>u</u>   <u>h</u>   <u>n</u>   <u>p</u>   <u>p</u>   <u>r</u></td></tr>
</table>

 Make Words: up   air   hair   pair   pain   rain   rein   pain   pear   ripe   ripen   upper   unripe   happier   unhappier

Directions: Tell the children how many letters to use to make each word.

- Emphasize how changing just one letter or rearranging letters makes different words:

    "Add a letter to **air** to spell the **hair**. His **hair** was red and curly."

    "Change 1 letter in **hair** to spell **pair**. Did you get a new **pair** of shoes?"

    "Change 1 letter in **rain** to spell **rein**. The rider pulled the **rein** to stop the horse."

- When the children are not just adding or changing one letter, cue them to start over:

    "Start over and use 4 letters to spell **pear**. The **pear** looked ripe and ready to eat."

- Give meaning or sentence clues when needed to clarify the word the students are making:

    "Use 3 letters to spell **air**. Outside the fresh **air** felt good."

- Give the children one minute to figure out the secret word and then give clues if needed:

    "Our secret word is related to the word **happy**."

 Sort Homophones: pear, **pair**; pane, **pain**; rein, **rain**

- Use a sentence to clarify meaning.

Sort Related Words: up, upper; ripe, ripen, unripe; happier, unhappier

- Use related words in a sentence that shows relationship. Talk about spelling change.

Sort Rhymes: (with same spelling patterns):

air	rain
hair	pain
pair	

 Transfer Related Words

- Have students use related words to spell **easier**, **prettier**, and **unhappy**.

Transfer Rhyming Patterns

- Have students use rhyming words to spell **brain**, **sprain**, **chain**, and **chair**.

Lesson 21
forgotten

Lesson Focus: suffix **en**
spelling change: double the **t** when adding **en**
homophones: **to, too**

Letters: e o o f g n r t t

 Make Words: to too net get got rot fog frog fret trot forget forgot rotten
gotten forgotten

Directions: Tell the children how many letters to use to make each word.

- Emphasize how changing just one letter or rearranging letters makes different words:

    "Add a letter to the word **to** and spell the word **too** like in **too** much."

    "Change 1 letter in **net** to spell **get**."

    "Add a letter to the word **fog** to spell the word **frog**."

- When the children are not just adding or changing one letter, cue them to start over:

    "Start over and use 4 letters to spell **trot**. The horse will **trot** around the track."

- Give meaning or sentence clues when needed to clarify the word the students are making:

    "Use 4 letters to spell **fret**. Don't **fret** over your mistakes."

- Give the children one minute to figure out the secret word and then give clues if needed:

    "Our secret word is related to the word **forget**."

 ## Sort Homophones: to, too

- Use a sentence to clarify meaning.

Sort Related Words: got, gotten; rot, rotten; forget, forgot, forgotten

- Use related words in a sentence that shows relationship. Talk about spelling change.

Sort Rhymes: (with same spelling patterns):

get	got	fog	gotten
net	rot	frog	rotten
fret	trot		forgotten
forget	forgot		

 ## Transfer Related Words

- Have students use **gotten**, **rotten**, and **forgotten** to spell **flatten**, **bitten**, and **written**.

Transfer Rhyming Patterns

- Have students use rhyming words to spell **blog**, **jog**, **clot**, and **plot**.

Lesson 22
clothes

Lesson Focus: homophones: **close, clothes**

Letters: e o c h l s t

 Make Words: set let lot hot hole sole shoe/hose those chose close stole hotel cloth closet clothes

Directions: Tell the children how many letters to use to make each word.

- Emphasize how changing just one letter or rearranging letters makes different words:

   "Change 1 letter in **set** to spell **let**."

   "Use the same letters in **shoe** to spell **hose**. I use the **hose** to wash my car."

   "Add 1 letter to **hose** to spell **those**. **Those** are the books I like to read."

- When the children are not just adding or changing one letter, cue them to start over:

   "Start over and use 5 letters to spell **stole**. The actress wore a fur **stole**."

- Give meaning or sentence clues when needed to clarify the word the students are making:

   "Use 4 letters to spell **hole**. The squirrel ran into the **hole** in the tree."

- Give the children one minute to figure out the secret word and then give clues if needed:

   "Our secret word is related to the word **cloth**."

 Sort Homophones: **close**, **clothes**

- Use a sentence to clarify meaning.

Sort Rhymes: (with same spelling patterns):

hose	lot	let	hole
close	hot	set	stole
those			sole
chose			

 Transfer Rhyming Patterns

- Have students use rhyming words to spell **pose**, **pole**, **mole**, **pot**, **pet**, and **rose**.

Lesson 23
everything

Lesson Focus: suffix **er**, meaning person or thing that does something
suffix **en**
spelling change: drop the **e** when adding **er** or **en**
homophones: **their**, **there**

Letters: e̲ e̲ i̲ g̲ h̲ n̲ r̲ t̲ v̲ y̲

 Make Words: try give giver given thing/night right three/there their every trying either neither everything

Directions: Tell the children how many letters to use to make each word.

- Emphasize how changing just one letter or rearranging letters makes different words:

    "Add a letter to **give** to spell the word **giver**. A person that gives is a **giver**."

    "Use the same letters in **thing** to spell **night**."

    "Change 1 letter in **night** to spell **right**."

- When the children are not just adding or changing one letter, cue them to start over:

    "Start over and use 5 letters to spell the number **three**."

- Give meaning or sentence clues when needed to clarify the word the students are making:

    "Use the same letters in **three** to spell **there**. I put it right over **there**."

- Give the children one minute to figure out the secret word and then give clues if needed:

    "Our secret word is a compound word and you spelled both words in the compound."

Sort Homophones: their there
- Use a sentence to clarify meaning.

Sort Related Words: give, giver, given; try, trying; every, thing, everything
- Use related words in a sentence that shows relationship. Talk about spelling change.

Sort Rhymes: (with same spelling patterns):

right	either
night	neither

 Transfer Related Words
- Have students use related words to spell **taken**, **driver**, and **driven**.

Transfer Rhyming Patterns
- Have students use rhyming words to spell **bright**, **fright**, **flight**, and **midnight**.

Lesson 24
airplanes

Lesson Focus: homophones: **pail**, **pale**; **sail**, **sale**; **pain**, **pane**; **rain**, **rein**; **pair**, **pear**; **plain**, **plane**

Letters: | a | a | e | i | l | p | n | r | s |

 Make Words: air pair pail sail sale pale pane pain rain rein pear plan plain plane airplanes

Directions: Tell the children how many letters to use to make each word.

- Emphasize how changing just one letter or rearranging letters makes different words:

   "Add a letter to **air** to spell the word **pair**."

   "Change 1 letter in **pair** to spell **pail**."

   "Add a letter to **plan** to spell **plain**. We will use **plain** paper, not lined paper."

- When the children are not just adding or changing one letter, cue them to start over:

   "Start over and use 4 letters to spell **pear**. One of my favorite fruits is a **pear**."

- Give meaning or sentence clues when needed to clarify the word the students are making:

   "Change one letter in **sale** to spell **pale**. The horse was not dark but a **pale** shade of brown."

- Give the children one minute to figure out the secret word and then give clues if needed:

   "Our secret word is related to the word **plane**."

 Sort Homophones: **pail**, **pale**; **sail**, **sale**; **pain**, **pane**; **rain**, **rein**; **pair**, **pear**; **plane**, **plane**

- Use a sentence with each one to clarify the meanings.

Sort Related Words: plane, airplanes

- Use related words in a sentence that shows relationship.

Sort Rhymes: (with same spelling patterns):

pale	air	pain	pane	pail
sale	pair	rain	plane	sail
		plain		

 Transfer Related Words

- Have students use related words to spell **airport**, **airline**, and **airwave**.

Transfer Rhyming Patterns

- Say the words **trail**, **whale**, **jail**, and **brain** and write each one using both possible patterns. Have the students decide which one looks right (**trail** or **trale**, **whale** or **whail**, **jail** or **jale**, **brain** or **brane**?) and have them spell it using only the pattern that looks right (**trail**, **whale**, **jail**, and **brain**).

Lesson 25

breakfast

Lesson Focus: suffix **er**, meaning person or thing that does something
suffix **er**, meaning more
spelling change: drop the **e** when adding **er**
homophones: **bare**, **bear**; **break**, **brake**; **stake**, steak

Letters: | a̲ | a̲ | e̲ | b̲ | f̲ | k̲ | r̲ | s̲ | t̲ |

 Make Words: fast bake bare/bear safe safer baker/brake/break steak/stake
stare faster breakfast

Directions: Tell the children how many letters to use to make each word.

- Emphasize how changing just one letter or rearranging letters makes different words:

    "Change 1 letter in **bake** to spell **bare**. I was standing there in my **bare** feet."

    "Use the same letters in **bare** to spell **bear**. The baby's favorite toy was a teddy **bear**."

    "Add a letter to **safe** to spell the word **safer**."

- When the children are not just adding or changing one letter, cue them to start over:

    "Start over and use 5 letters to spell **baker**. A person who bakes is a **baker**."

- Give meaning or sentence clues when needed to clarify the word the students are making:

    "Change one letter to spell **stare**. I know it is not nice to **stare** at people."

- Give the children one minute to figure out the secret word and then give clues if needed:

    "Our secret word is something we eat."

 Sort Homophones: bare, bear; break, brake; stake, steak

- Use a sentence to clarify meaning.

Sort Related Words: bake, baker; safe, safer; fast, faster

- Use related words in a sentence that shows relationship. Talk about spelling change.

Sort Rhymes: (with same spelling patterns):

bare	break	brake
stare	steak	stake
		bake

 Transfer Related Words

- Have students use related words to spell **later**, **harder**, and **player**.

Transfer Rhyming Patterns

- Tell students that **break** and **steak** are the exceptions. Almost all other words that rhyme are spelled with the a-**k**-e pattern. Have students use rhyming words to spell **snake**, **flake**, **wake**, and **quake**.

Lesson 26

couldn't

Lesson Focus: prefix **un**, meaning opposite
contractions: **don't**, **couldn't**

Letters: o u c d l n t '

 Make Words: do not cot old cold told undo don't loud cloud/could
donut untold couldn't

Directions: Tell the children how many letters to use to make each word.

• Emphasize how changing just one letter or rearranging letters makes different words:

"Change 1 letter in **not** to spell **cot**. Have you ever slept on a **cot**?"

"Add a letter to **old** to spell **cold**."

"Use the same letters in **cloud** to spell **could**. He **could** do that."

• When the children are not just adding or changing one letter, cue them to start over:

"Start over and use 5 letters to spell **donut**."

• Remind the students that the apostrophe will be used for words that are contractions. When you ask them to spell the 4 letter word **don't**, make sure they use the apostrophe.

• Give meaning or sentence clues when needed to clarify the word the students are making:

"Use 4 letters to spell **undo**. I cannot **undo** this knot!"

• Give the children one minute to figure out the secret word and then give clues if needed:

"Our secret word is a contraction."

 Sort Contractions: **couldn't, don't**

• Have students tell what words make up the contractions.

Sort Related Words: **told, untold; do, undo**

• Use related words in a sentence that shows relationship.

Sort Rhymes: (with same spelling patterns):

loud	not	old
cloud	cot	cold
		told

 Transfer Related Words

• Have students use related words to spell **unfair**, **unjust**, and **unlock**.

Transfer Rhyming Patterns

• Have students use rhyming words to spell **proud**, **sold**, **scold**, and **bold**.

Lesson 27
shouldn't

Lesson Focus: prefix **un**, meaning opposite
contractions **don't, shouldn't**
homophones: **sun, son**

Letters: | o u d h l n s t ' |

 Make Words: do not sun son out old sold don't shout/south sound
hound unsold should shouldn't

> **Directions:** Tell the children how many letters to use to make each word.

- Emphasize how changing just one letter or rearranging letters makes different words:

  "Change 1 letter in **sun** to spell **son**. I have a **son**."

  "Add a letter to **old** to spell **sold**. They **sold** their house to buy a new one."

  "Use the same letters in **shout** to spell **south**."

- When the children are not just adding or changing one letter, cue them to start over:

  "Start over and use 5 letters to spell **sound**."

- Remind the students that the apostrophe will be used for words that are contractions. When you ask them to spell the 4 letter word **don't**, make sure they use the apostrophe.

- Give meaning or sentence clues when needed to clarify the word the students are making:

  "Use 6 letters to spell **unsold**. Something that is not sold is **unsold**."

- Give the children one minute to figure out the secret word and then give clues if needed:

  "Our secret word is a contraction."

 ## Sort Contractions: shouldn't, don't

- Have students tell what words make up the contractions.

Sort Homophones: sun, son

- Give a sentence to make the meaning clear.

Sort Related Words: sold, unsold

- Use related words in a sentence that shows relationship.

Sort Rhymes: (with same spelling patterns):
| hound | out | old |
| sound | shout | sold |

 ## Transfer Related Words

- Have students use related words to spell **unkind, undress,** and **unlucky.**

Transfer Rhyming Patterns

- Have students use rhyming words to spell **pout, scout, ground,** and **playground.**

Lesson 28

wouldn't

Lesson Focus: prefix **un**, meaning opposite
contractions: **won't**, **wouldn't**
homophones: **would**, **wood** (included in next lesson)

Letters: | o u d l n t w ' |

 Make Words: do dot not now/own/won down town undo told won't donut would untold wouldn't

Directions: Tell the children how many letters to use to make each word.

- Emphasize how changing just one letter or rearranging letters makes different words:

    "Add a letter to **do** to spell **dot**."

    "Change 1 letter in **dot** to spell **not**."

    "Use the same letters in **now** to spell **own** (and then **won**)."

- When the children are not just adding or changing one letter, cue them to start over:

    "Start over and use 5 letters to spell **down**."

- Remind the students that the apostrophe will be used for words that are contractions. When you ask them to spell the 4 letter word **won't**, make sure they use the apostrophe.

- Give meaning or sentence clues when needed to clarify the word the students are making:

    "Use 5 letters to spell **would**. I **would** like to go to the ballgame tonight."

- Give the children one minute to figure out the secret word and then give clues if needed:

    "Our secret word is another contraction."

 Sort Contractions: wouldn't, won't

- Have students tell what words make up the contractions.

Sort Related Words: told, untold; do, undo

- Use related words in a sentence that shows relationship.

Sort Rhymes: (with same spelling patterns):

down	not
town	dot

 Transfer Related Words

- Have students use related words to spell **unhappy**, **untie**, and **unpack**.

Transfer Rhyming Patterns

- Have students use rhyming words to spell **crown**, **clown**, **frown**, and **drown**.

Lesson 29

countdown

Lesson Focus: homophones: **to, two, too; wood, would**
(included in previous lesson)

Letters: o o u c d n n t w

 Make Words: do to too two cow now down town noon noun outdo wound count countdown

Directions: Tell the children how many letters to use to make each word.

- Emphasize how changing just one letter or rearranging letters makes different words:

    "Add a letter to **to** and spell the word **too** like **too** much!"

    "Change 1 letter in **cow** to spell **now**."

    "Change 1 letter in **down** to spell **town**."

- When the children are not just adding or changing one letter, cue them to start over:

    "Start over and use 4 letters to spell **noon**."

- Give meaning or sentence clues when needed to clarify the word the students are making:

    "Use 4 letters to spell **noun**. A **noun** is a person, place, or thing."

- Give the children one minute to figure out the secret word and then give clues if needed:

    "Our secret word is a compound word combining two words we made."

 Sort Homophones: **to, too, two; wood, would** (from previous lesson)

- Give a sentence to make the meaning clear.

Sort Related Words: **do, outdo**

- Use related words in a sentence that shows relationship.

Sort Rhymes: (with same spelling patterns):

down	**cow**
town	**now**

 Transfer Related Words

- Have students use related words to spell **outshine**, **outgrow**, and **outnumber**.

Transfer Rhyming Patterns

- Have students use rhyming words to spell **chow**, **plow**, **downtown**, and **touchdown**.

Lesson 30
powerful

Lesson Focus: suffix **ful**

homophones: **for, four; flour, flower**

Letters: | e | o | u | f | l | p | r | w |

 Make Words: low/owl few for four flew flow/wolf plow prowl power flour flower powerful

Directions: Tell the children how many letters to use to make each word.

- Emphasize how changing just one letter or rearranging letters makes different words:

  "Use the same letters in **low** to spell **owl**."

  "Add a letter to **for** to spell the number **four**."

  "Change 1 letter in **flew** to spell **flow**. We watched the water **flow** into the stream."

  "Use the same letters in **flow** to spell **wolf**."

- When the children are not just adding or changing one letter, cue them to start over:

  "Start over and use 4 letters to spell **plow**."

- Give meaning or sentence clues when needed to clarify the word the students are making:

  "Use 5 letters to spell **prowl**. Some animals like to **prowl** at night."

- Give the children one minute to figure out the secret word and then give clues if needed:

  "Our secret word is related to the word **power**."

 Sort Homophones: **for, four; flour, flower**

- Give a sentence to make the meaning clear.

Sort Related Words: **power, powerful**

- Use related words in a sentence that shows relationship.

Sort Rhymes: (with same spelling patterns):

low	few	owl	power
flow	flew	prowl	flower

 Transfer Related Words

- Have students use related words to spell **cheerful**, **thankful**, and **painful**.

Transfer Rhyming Patterns

- Have students use rhyming words to spell **howl**, **growl**, **tower**, and **shower**.

Lesson 31
wonderful

Lesson Focus: suffix **ful**
suffix **er**, meaning person or thing that does something
prefix **un**, meaning opposite
homophones: **won**, **one**; **flour**, **flower**

Letters: | e o u d f l n r w |

 Make Words: won/own   one   old   fold   round   found   owner   flour   flower
folder   unfold   wonder   founder   wonderful

Directions: Tell the children how many letters to use to make each word.

- Emphasize how changing just one letter or rearranging letters makes different words:

   "Use the same letters in **won** to spell **own**."

   "Add a letter to **old** to spell **fold**. Do you ever help **fold** the clothes?"

   "Change 1 letter in **round** to spell **found**."

- When the children are not just adding or changing one letter, cue them to start over:

   "Start over and use 5 letters to spell **owner**."

- Give meaning or sentence clues when needed to clarify the word the students are making:

   "Use 5 letters to spell **flour**. The recipe called for 2 cups of **flour**."

- Give the children one minute to figure out the secret word and then give clues if needed:

   "Our secret word is related to the word **wonder**."

Sort Homophones: won, one; flour, flower

- Use a sentence to clarify meaning.

Sort Related Words: **wonder, wonderful; own, owner; found, founder;
fold, unfold, folder**

- Use related words in a sentence that shows relationship.

Sort Rhymes: (with same spelling patterns):

| round | old |
| found | fold |

 Transfer Related Words

- Have students use related words to spell **useful**, **worker**, and **unpack**.

Transfer Rhyming Patterns

- Have students use rhyming words to spell **sound**, **ground**, **bound**, and **rebound**.

Lesson 32

carefully

Lesson Focus: suffixes **ful**, **ly**, **y**
prefix **re**, meaning back

Letters: | a | e | u | c | f | l | l | r | y |

 Make Words: call fall fell yell real care curl curly cruel clear recall really clearly careful carefully

Directions: Tell the children how many letters to use to make each word.

- Emphasize how changing just one letter or rearranging letters makes different words:

    "Change 1 letter in **call** to spell **fall**."

    "Change just one letter in **fall** to spell **fell**. The small child **fell** down."

    "Add a letter to **curl** to spell **curly**."

- When the children are not just adding or changing one letter, cue them to start over:

    "Start over and use 5 letters to spell **cruel**."

- Give meaning or sentence clues when needed to clarify the word the students are making:

    "Use 6 letters to spell **really**. He is a **really** good friend."

- Give the children one minute to figure out the secret word and then give clues if needed:

    "Our secret word is related to the word **care**."

 Sort Related Words: **curl**, **curly**; **real**, **really**; **clear**, **clearly**; **call**, **recall**; **care**, **careful**, **carefully**

- Use related words in a sentence that shows relationship.

Sort Rhymes: (with same spelling patterns):

fall	**fell**
call	**yell**

 Transfer Related Words

- Have students use related words to spell **quickly**, **slowly**, and **nearly**.

Transfer Rhyming Patterns

- Have students use rhyming words to spell **baseball**, **meatball**, **retell**, and **doorbell**.

Lesson 33

thankless

Lesson Focus: suffixes **en**, **less**
spelling change: drop final **e** when adding **en**

Letters: | a | e | h | k | l | n | s | s | t |

 Make Words: hat Hank tank talk leak leash stalk thank ankle sneak/snake shake shaken hatless thankless

Directions: Tell the children how many letters to use to make each word.

- Emphasize how changing just one letter or rearranging letters makes different words:

    "Change a letter in **tank** to spell **talk**."

    "Use the same letters in **sneak** to spell **snake**."

    "Add a letter to **shake** to spell **shaken**."

- When the children are not just adding or changing one letter, cue them to start over:

    "Start over and use 6 letters to spell **hatless**."

- Give meaning or sentence clues when needed to clarify the word the students are making:

    "Use 5 letters to spell **ankle**. I twisted my **ankle** when I slipped on the stairs."

- Give the children one minute to figure out the secret word and then give clues if needed:

    "Our secret word is related to the word **thank**."

 Sort Related Words: shake, shaken; hat, hatless; thank, thankless

- Use related words in a sentence that shows relationship.

Sort Rhymes: (with same spelling patterns):

leak	talk	tank	snake
sneak	stalk	Hank	shake
		thank	

 Transfer Related Words

- Have students use related words to spell **endless**, **harmless**, and **wireless**.

Transfer Rhyming Patterns

- Have students use rhyming words to spell **peak**, **speak**, **prank**, and **sidewalk**.

Lesson 34

carelessly

Lesson Focus: suffixes **less**, **ly**, **y**
prefix **re**, meaning back
spelling change: drop final **e** when adding **y**

Letters: | a e e c l l r s s y |

Make Words: less real care/race lace call clear scare scary recess recall really clearly careless carelessly

Directions: Tell the children how many letters to use to make each word.

- Emphasize how changing just one letter or rearranging letters makes different words:

  "Use the same letters in **care** to spell **race**."

  "Change 1 letter in **race** to spell **lace**. Please tie your shoe **lace**."

  "Change a letter in **scare** to spell the **scary**."

- When the children are not just adding or changing one letter, cue them to start over:

  "Start over and use 6 letters to spell **recess**."

- Give meaning or sentence clues when needed to clarify the word the students are making:

  "Use 6 letters to spell **recall**. When something goes back to where it is made, it is called a **recall**. Once, they had to **recall** a certain kind of peanut butter."

- Give the children one minute to figure out the secret word and then give clues if needed:

  "Our secret word is related to the word **care**."

Sort Related Words: **scare, scary; real, really; clear, clearly; call, recall; care, careless, carelessly**

- Use related words in a sentence that shows relationship.

Sort Rhymes: (with same spelling patterns):

race	care	less
lace	scare	recess
		careless

Transfer Related Words

- Have students use related words to spell **useless**, **helpless**, and **helplessly**.

Transfer Rhyming Patterns

- Have students use rhyming words to spell **press**, **impress**, **place**, and **replace**.

Lesson 35
paperweight

Lesson Focus: homophones: **ate**, **eight**; **rap**, **wrap**; **right**, **write**; **wait**, **weight**

Letters: | a | e | e | i | g | h | p | p | r | t | w |

Make Words: ate   rat   rap   wrap   trap   wart   wait   page   rage   paper   right   write   eight   weight   paperweight

Directions: Tell the children how many letters to use to make each word.

- Emphasize how changing just one letter or rearranging letters makes different words:

    "Add a letter to **rap** to spell the **wrap** that you do with a birthday present."

    "Change 1 letter in **wart** to spell **wait**."

    "Add a letter to **eight** and you can spell **weight**. What is your **weight**?"

- When the children are not just adding or changing one letter, cue them to start over:

    "Start over and use 4 letters to spell **page**."

- Give meaning or sentence clues when needed to clarify the word the students are making:

    "Use 3 letters to spell **rap**. I knew the **rap** song he was singing."

- Give the children one minute to figure out the secret word and then give clues if needed:

    "Our secret word is a compound word combining two words we made."

Sort Homophones: ate, eight; rap, wrap; right, write; wait, weight

- Give a sentence to make the meaning clear.

Sort Related Words: paper, weight, paperweight

- Use related words in a sentence that shows relationship.

Sort Rhymes: (with same spelling patterns):

rap	**page**
wrap	**rage**
trap	

Transfer Related Words

- Have students use related words to spell **paperclip**, **paperback**, and **weightless**.

Transfer Rhyming Patterns

- Have students use rhyming words to spell **cage**, **wage**, **stage**, and **kidnap**.

Lesson 36
vacations

Lesson Focus: suffix **tion**

Letters: | a | a | i | o | c | n | s | t | v |

 Make Words: cats/acts/cast   vast/vats   coats/coast/tacos   sonic   tonic   casino   action   vacant   vacations

Directions: Tell the children how many letters to use to make each word.

- Emphasize how changing just one letter or rearranging letters makes different words:

    "Use the same letters in **cats** to spell **acts**."

    "Use these same letters again to spell **cast**."

    "Change 1 letter in **sonic** to spell **tonic**. The bottle of liquid was labeled **tonic**."

- When the children are not just adding or changing one letter, cue them to start over:

    "Start over and use 6 letters to spell **casino**."

- Give meaning or sentence clues when needed to clarify the word the students are making:

    "Use 6 letters to spell **vacant**. When a house is empty we say it is **vacant**."

- Give the children one minute to figure out the secret word and then give clues if needed:

    "Our secret word is related to vacant—but it is something we all enjoy."

 Sort Related Words: **acts, action; vacant, vacations**

- Use related words in a sentence that shows relationship.

Sort Rhymes: (with same spelling patterns):

cats	cast	sonic
vats	vast	tonic

 Transfer Related Words

- Have students use related words to spell **invention**, **collection**, and **promotion**.

Transfer Rhyming Patterns

- Have students use rhyming words to spell **past**, **blast**, **newscast**, and **contrast**.

Lesson 37
connections

Lesson Focus: suffixes **tion**, **est**
homophones: **sent**, **cent**, **scent**

Letters: <u>e</u>   <u>i</u>   <u>o</u>   <u>o</u>   <u>c</u>   <u>c</u>   <u>n</u>   <u>n</u>   <u>n</u>   <u>s</u>   <u>t</u>

 Make Words: sit   set   net   ice   nice   sent   cent   scent   nicest/insect   notion   section   consent   connect   connections

Directions: Tell the children how many letters to use to make each word.

- Emphasize how changing just one letter or rearranging letters makes different words:

  "Change 1 letter in **sit** to spell **set**."

  "Add a letter to **ice** to spell the **nice**."

  "Use the same letters in **nicest** to spell **insect**."

- When the children are not just adding or changing one letter, cue them to start over:

  "Start over and use 6 letters to spell **notion**. I had a **notion** it was her."

- Give meaning or sentence clues when needed to clarify the word the students are making:

  "Use 7 letters now to spell **consent**. You need your parent's **consent** to go on the trip."

- Give the children one minute to figure out the secret word and then give clues if needed:

  "Our secret word is related to the word **connect**."

 Sort Homophones: sent, cent, scent

- Give a sentence to make the meaning clear.

Sort Related Words: nice, nicest; connect, connections

- Use related words in a sentence that shows relationship.

Sort Rhymes: (with same spelling patterns):

set	ice	sent	insect
net	nice	cent	connect
		scent	
		consent	

 Transfer Related Words

- Have students use related words to spell **collections**, **corrections**, and **objections**.

Transfer Rhyming Patterns

- Have students use rhyming words to spell **protect**, **perfect**, **inspect**, and **expect**.

Lesson 38

expression

Lesson Focus: suffixes **sion**, **en**, **er**, **ness**
prefix **re**, meaning again
spelling change: **es** is added when words end in **x**

Letters: e   e   i   o   n   p   r   s   s   x

 Make Words: six nix open nose rose ripe ripen sixes nixes opener/reopen
expose express ripeness expression

Directions: Tell the children how many letters to use to make each word.

- Emphasize how changing just one letter or rearranging letters makes different words:

  "Change 1 letter in the word **six** to spell **nix**. I would like to invite the whole class to my party, but I know my mom would **nix** that plan."

  "Add 1 letter to the word **ripe** to spell **ripen**. The banana will **ripen** in a day or two."

  "Use the same letters in **opener** to spell **reopen**."

- When the children are not just adding or changing one letter, cue them to start over:

  "Start over and use 6 letters to spell **expose**. Do not **expose** this plant to sunlight."

- Give meaning or sentence clues when needed to clarify the word the students are making:

  "Use 7 letters to spell **express**. Try to **express** your ideas clearly when you write."

- Give the children one minute to figure out the secret word and then give clues if needed:

  "Our secret word is related to the word **express**."

 Sort Related Words: **six, sixes; nix, nixes; ripe, ripen, ripeness;**
open, reopen, opener; express, expression

- Use related words in a sentence that shows relationship.

Sort Rhymes: (with same spelling patterns):

six	**sixes**	**rose**
nix	**nixes**	**nose**
		expose

Transfer Related Words

- Have students use related words to spell **impression**, **depression**, and **kindness**.

Transfer Rhyming Patterns

- Have students use rhyming words to spell **fix**, **fixes**, **mix**, and **mixes**.

Lesson 39
returning

Lesson Focus: suffix **er**, meaning person or thing that does something
spelling change: double the **n** when adding **er**
prefix **re**, meaning back or again
prefix **un**, meaning opposite

Letters: e   i   u   g   n   n   r   r   t

Make Words: tie   gun   run   runt/turn   untie/unite   grunt   rerun   runner
gunner   urgent   return   turning   returning

Directions: Tell the children how many letters to use to make each word.

- Emphasize how changing just one letter or rearranging letters makes different words:

  "Change 1 letter in **gun** to spell **run**."

  "Add a letter to **run** to spell **runt**. The smallest kitten is called the **runt** of the litter."

  "Use the same letters in **runt** to spell **turn**."

- When the children are not just adding or changing one letter, cue them to start over:

  "Start over and use 5 letters to spell **untie**."

- Give meaning or sentence clues when needed to clarify the word the students are making:

  "Use the same letters to spell the word **unite**. **Unite** means to join together."

- Give the children one minute to figure out the secret word and then give clues if needed:

  "Our secret word is related to the word **return**."

Sort Related Words: tie, untie; run, rerun, runner; gun, gunner;
turn, turning; return, returning

- Use related words in a sentence that shows relationship.

Sort Rhymes: (with same spelling patterns):

runt	run	runner
grunt	gun	gunner

Transfer Related Words

- Have students use related words to spell **refill**, **rebuild**, and **repaint**.

Transfer Rhyming Patterns

- Have students use rhyming words to spell **stun**, **stunt**, **bun**, and **bunt**.

rewriting

Lesson Focus: prefix **re**, meaning again
suffix **er**, meaning person or thing that does something
spelling change: drop the **e** when adding **er** or **ing**

Letters: | e | i | i | g | n | r | r | t | w |

 Make Words: ring   wing   twin   twig   wire   tire   write   writer   ringer   tiring   wiring   writing   rewiring   rewriting

Directions: Tell the children how many letters to use to make each word.

- Emphasize how changing just one letter or rearranging letters makes different words:

  "Change a letter in **ring** to spell **wing**."

  "Change just one letter in **wire** to spell **tire**."

  "Add a letter to **write** to spell **writer**."

- When the children are not just adding or changing one letter, cue them to start over:

  "Start over and use 6 letters to spell **ringer**."

- Give meaning or sentence clues when needed to clarify the word the students are making:

  "Use 6 letters to spell **tiring**. I missed the bus and the walk all the way home from school was very **tiring**."

- Give the children one minute to figure out the secret word and then give clues if needed:

  "Our secret word is related to the word **write**."

 Sort Related Words: ring, ringer; tire, tiring; wire, wiring, rewiring;
write, writer, writing, rewriting

- Use related words in a sentence that shows relationship.

Sort Rhymes: (with same spelling patterns):

ring	wire	tiring
wing	tire	wiring
		rewiring

 Transfer Related Words

- Have students use related words to spell **mover**, **remover**, and **rebuilding**.

Transfer Rhyming Patterns

- Have students use rhyming words to spell **fire**, **firing**, **hire**, and **hiring**.

Lesson 41
knowledge

Lesson Focus: suffix **en**
homophones: **no, know; new, knew**

Letters: <u>e</u> <u>e</u> <u>o</u> <u>d</u> <u>g</u> <u>k</u> <u>l</u> <u>n</u> <u>w</u>

Make Words: no now new old gold knee knew know edge wedge ledge
kneel olden golden knowledge

Directions: Tell the children how many letters to use to make each word.

- Emphasize how changing just one letter or rearranging letters makes different words:

    "Add a letter to **old** to spell the color word **gold**."

    "Change 1 letter in **knee** to spell **knew**. I **knew** the answer to every question!"

    "Add a letter to **edge** to spell the word **wedge**. He used a metal **wedge** to chop the wood into pieces just right for the fireplace."

- When the children are not just adding or changing one letter, cue them to start over:

    "Start over and use 5 letters to spell **kneel**. If you **kneel** down you can see under that cabinet."

- Give meaning or sentence clues when needed to clarify the word the students are making:

    "Change just one letter in **wedge** and you can spell **ledge**. The bird sat on the window **ledge**."

- Give the children one minute to figure out the secret word and then give clues if needed:

    "Our secret word is related to the words **know (k-n-o-w)** and **knew (k-n-e-w)**."

Sort Homophones: no, know; new, knew

- Use sentences to clarify meaning.

Sort Related Words: know, knew, knowledge; knee, kneel; old, olden; gold, golden

- Use related words in a sentence that shows relationship.

Sort Rhymes: (with same spelling patterns):

new	edge	old	olden
knew	wedge	gold	golden
	ledge		
	knowledge		

Transfer Related Words

- Have students use **olden** and **golden** to spell **eaten, beaten,** and **wooden**.

Transfer Rhyming Patterns

- Have students use rhyming words to spell **flew, grew, scold,** and **pledge**.

Lesson 42
blueberry

Lesson Focus: suffix **er**, meaning person or thing that does something
suffix **y**
spelling change: drop final **e** when adding **er**
homophones: **by**, **buy**; **bury**, **berry**

Letters: e e u b b l r r y

 Make Words: by buy bee Lee/eel reel blue rule bury berry buyer ruler rubber rubbery blueberry

Directions: Tell the children how many letters to use to make each word.

- Emphasize how changing just one letter or rearranging letters makes different words:
  "Add a letter to **by** to spell the **buy** that you do at the store."
  "Change 1 letter in **bee** to spell the name **Lee**."
  "Add a letter to **rubber** to spell the word **rubbery**. I don't like foods that taste **rubbery**."

- When the children are not just adding or changing one letter, cue them to start over:
  "Start over and use 4 letters to spell **bury**. I helped my dad dig a hole to **bury** our old dog in the back yard."

- Give meaning or sentence clues when needed to clarify the word the students are making:
  "Use five letters to spell the **berry** you can pick and eat."

- Give the children one minute to figure out the secret word and then give clues if needed:
  "Our secret word is a compound word made up of two words you already made."

 Sort Homophones: by, buy; bury, berry

- Use sentences to clarify meaning.

Sort Related Words: blue, berry, blueberry; rule, ruler; buy, buyer

- Use related words in a sentence that shows relationship.

Sort Rhymes: (with same spelling patterns):

eel	Lee
reel	bee

 Transfer Related Words

- Have students use related words to spell **strawberry**, **blackberry**, and **cranberry**.

Transfer Rhyming Patterns

- Have students use rhyming words to spell **feel**, **free**, **flee**, and **agree**.

Lesson 43
creatures

Lesson Focus: suffixes **ure**, **er**

spelling change: drop final **e** when adding **er**, **ure**

Letters: a e e u c r r s t

Make Words: sue/use user rate race racer rater trace/crate create

tracer secret rescue rescuer creatures

Directions: Tell the children how many letters to use to make each word.

- Emphasize how changing just one letter or rearranging letters makes different words:

    "Use the same letters in **sue** to spell **use**."

    "Add a letter to **use** to spell the word **user**. A person who uses something is a **user**."

    "Change 1 letter in **rate** to spell **race**."

    "Use the same letters in **trace** to spell **crate**."

- When the children are not just adding or changing one letter, cue them to start over:

    "Start over and use 6 letters to spell **secret**."

- Give meaning or sentence clues when needed to clarify the word the students are making:

    "Use 6 letters to spell **rescue**. We watched the **rescue** on television."

- Give the children one minute to figure out the secret word and then give clues if needed:

    "Our secret word is related to the word **create**."

Sort Related Words: use, user; race, racer; rate, rater; trace, tracer; rescue, rescuer; create, creatures

- Use related words in a sentence that shows relationship.

Sort Rhymes: (with same spelling patterns):

race	racer	rate	sue
trace	tracer	crate	rescue

Transfer Related Words

- Have students use related words to spell **writer**, **driver**, and **mixture**.

Transfer Rhyming Patterns

- Have students use rhyming words to spell **clue**, **rotate**, **place**, and **fireplace**.

Lesson 44
departure

Lesson Focus: suffixes **ure**, **er**
spelling change: drop final **e** when adding **er**, **ure**
prefix **re**, meaning again
homophones: **deer**, **dear**

Letters: <u>a</u>   <u>e</u>   <u>e</u>   <u>u</u>   <u>d</u>   <u>p</u>   <u>r</u>   <u>r</u>   <u>t</u>

 Make Words: eat/ate   ape   tape   date   read/dear   deer   trade   trader   reader/reread   update   depart   departure

Directions: Tell the children how many letters to use to make each word.

- Emphasize how changing just one letter or rearranging letters makes different words:

    "Use the same letters in **eat** to spell **ate**."

    "Change 1 letter in **ate** to spell **ape**. An **ape** is an animal."

    "Add a letter to **ape** to spell **tape**. I can **tape** those pieces together."

- When the children are not just adding or changing one letter, cue them to start over:

    "Start over and use 4 letters to spell **read**. I like to **read** books."

- Give meaning or sentence clues when needed to clarify the word the students are making:

    "Use the same letters to spell the word **dear**, like you use to start a letter."

- Give the children one minute to figure out the secret word and then give clues if needed:

    "Our secret word is related to the word **depart**."

 ## Sort Homophones: dear, deer

- Give a sentence to make the meaning clear.

Sort Related Words: date, update; read, reader, reread; trade, trader; depart, departure

- Use related words in a sentence that shows relationship.

Sort Rhymes: (with same spelling patterns):

ate	ape
date	tape
update	

 ## Transfer Related Words

- Have students use related words to spell **picture**, **nature**, and **future**.

Transfer Rhyming Patterns

- Have students use rhyming words to spell **grape**, **shape**, **scrape**, and **escape**.

pleasure

Lesson Focus: suffix **ure**
spelling change: drop final **e** when adding **ure**
prefix **re**, meaning back

Letters: | a | e | e | u | l | p | r | s |

 Make Words: use sure pure sale/seal real seep sleep super reuse
reseal resale asleep/please pleasure

Directions: Tell the children how many letters to use to make each word.

- Emphasize how changing just one letter or rearranging letters makes different words:

    "Change 1 letter in **sure** to spell **pure**. Something that is free from anything bad is said to be **pure**."

    "Use the same letters in **sale** to spell **seal**. **Seal** the envelope and then mail it."

    "Add a letter to **seep** to spell **sleep**."

- When the children are not just adding or changing one letter, cue them to start over:

    "Start over and use 5 letters to spell **super**. You are doing a **super** job."

- Give meaning or sentence clues when needed to clarify the word the students are making:

    "Use 5 letters to spell **reuse**. When you use something again, you **reuse** it."

- Give the children one minute to figure out the secret word and then give clues if needed:

    "Our secret word is related to the word **please**."

 Sort Related Words: use, reuse; seal, reseal; sale, resale; sleep, asleep;
please, pleasure

- Use related words in a sentence that shows relationship.

Sort Rhymes: (with same spelling patterns):

seep	seal	sure
sleep	real	pure
asleep	reseal	pleasure

 Transfer Related Words

- Have students use related words to spell **awake**, **measure**, and **treasure**.

Transfer Rhyming Patterns

- Have students use rhyming words to spell **jeep**, **creep**, **steep**, and **sweep**.

Lesson 46

acceptable

Homophones **accept** and **except** are included in this lesson and the following lesson.

Lesson Focus: suffix **able**
homophones: **be**, **bee**; **beet**, **beat**

Letters: a a e e b c c l p t

 Make Words: be bee beet beat late lace able table cable plate place peace accept capable acceptable

Directions: Tell the children how many letters to use to make each word.

- Emphasize how changing just one letter or rearranging letters makes different words:

    "Add a letter to **be** to spell the **bee** that is an insect."

    "Change 1 letter in **beet** to spell **beat**. I like the **beat** of that music."

    "Add a letter to **able** to spell **table**."

- When the children are not just adding or changing one letter, cue them to start over:

    "Start over and use 5 letters to spell **plate**."

- Give meaning or sentence clues when needed to clarify the word the students are making:

    "Use 6 letters to spell **accept**. I will **accept** your gift."

- Give the children one minute to figure out the secret word and then give clues if needed:

    "Our secret word is related to the word **accept**."

 Sort Homophones: be, bee; beet, beat

- Give a sentence to make the meaning clear.

Sort Related Words: accept, acceptable

- Use related words in a sentence that shows relationship.

Sort Rhymes: (with same spelling patterns):

lace	late	able
place	plate	table
		cable

 Transfer Related Words

- Have students use related words to spell **readable**, **laughable**, and **favorable**.

Transfer Rhyming Patterns

- Have students use rhyming words to spell **space**, **trace**, **brace**, and **embrace**.

Lesson 47
exceptions

Homophones **accept** and **except** are included in this lesson and the preceding lesson.

Lesson Focus: suffix **tion**
homophones: **except**, **accept** (from previous lesson)

Letters: <u>e</u>   <u>e</u>   <u>i</u>   <u>o</u>   <u>c</u>   <u>n</u>   <u>p</u>   <u>s</u>   <u>t</u>   <u>x</u>

 Make Words: six   nose   pose   exit   exist   spite   excite   expose   except/expect
insect   inspect   sixteen   coexist   exceptions

Directions: Tell the children how many letters to use to make each word.

- Emphasize how changing just one letter or rearranging letters makes different words:

    "Change 1 letter in **nose** to spell **pose**. Will you **pose** for a picture?"

    "Add 1 letter to **exit** to spell the word **exist**. We all **exist**."

    "Use the same letters in **except** to spell **expect**."

- When the children are not just adding or changing one letter, cue them to start over:

    "Start over and use 6 letters to spell **insect**."

- Give meaning or sentence clues when needed to clarify the word the students are making:

    "Add a letter to spell **inspect**. If you look at something carefully, you **inspect** it."

- Give the children one minute to figure out the secret word and then give clues if needed:

    "Our secret word is related to the word **except**."

 Sort Homophones: except, accept (from previous lesson)

- Give a sentence to make the meaning clear.

Sort Related Words: pose, expose; six, sixteen; exist, coexist; except, exceptions

- Use related words in a sentence that shows relationship.

Sort Rhymes: (with same spelling patterns):

nose	spite	insect
pose	excite	inspect
expose		expect

Transfer Related Words

- Have students use related words to spell **export**, **exchange**, and **explore**.

Transfer Rhyming Patterns

- Have students use rhyming words to spell **defect**, **select**, **perfect**, and **subject**.

Lesson 48
whatever

Homophones **weather** and **whether** are included in this lesson and the following lesson.

Lesson Focus: suffix **er**, meaning person or thing that does something
prefix **re**, meaning back
homophones: **hear, here**

Letters: | a | e | e | h | r | t | v | w |

 Make Words: eat ear hear heat/hate what rave wave here ever eater heater/reheat weather whatever

Directions: Tell the children how many letters to use to make each word.

- Emphasize how changing just one letter or rearranging letters makes different words:
  "Change 1 letter in **eat** to spell **ear**."
  "Add 1 letter to **ear** to spell **hear**. We **hear** with our ear."
  "Use the same letters in **heat** to spell **hate**. I **hate** to make mistakes."

- When the children are not just adding or changing one letter, cue them to start over:
  "Start over and use 4 letters to spell **here**. Your seat is right **here**."

- Give meaning or sentence clues when needed to clarify the word the students are making:
  "Change one letter in **wave** to spell **rave**. Everyone will **rave** when they taste your cookies."

- Give the children one minute to figure out the secret word and then give clues if needed:
  "Our secret word is a compound word combining two words we made."

 Sort Homophones: **hear, here**

- Use a sentence to clarify meaning.

Sort Related Words: **eat, eater; heat, heater, reheat**

- Use related words in a sentence that shows relationship. Talk about spelling change.

Sort Rhymes: (with same spelling patterns):

| rate | rave | ear | eat | eater |
| hate | wave | hear | heat | heater |

Transfer Related Words

- Have students use related words to spell **refill**, **filler**, and **baker**.

Transfer Rhyming Patterns

- Have students use rhyming words to spell **shave**, **grave**, **brave**, and **slave**.

Lesson 49
whether

Homophones **weather** and **whether** are included in this lesson and the preceding lesson.

Homophones **threw** and **through** are included in this lesson and the following lesson.

Lesson Focus: homophones: we, wee; **whether**, **weather** (from previous lesson)

Letters: | e | e | h | h | r | t | w |

 Make Words: he we wee her the wet were here tree three/there where threw whether

Directions: Tell the children how many letters to use to make each word.

- Emphasize how changing just one letter or rearranging letters makes different words:

    "Add a letter to **we** to spell the **wee** that means very small."

    "Change 1 letter in **were** to spell **here**."

    "Use the same letters in **three** to spell **there**."

- When the children are not just adding or changing one letter, cue them to start over:

    "Start over and use 5 letters to spell **threw**. He **threw** the ball."

- Give meaning or sentence clues when needed to clarify the word the students are making:

    "Change 1 letter to spell **where**. **Where** are you going?"

- Give the children one minute to figure out the secret word and then give clues if needed:

    "Our secret word is a homophone for w-e-a-t-h-e-r."

 Sort Homophones: we, wee; **whether**, **weather** (from previous lesson)

- Give a sentence to make the meaning clear.

Sort Rhymes: (with same spelling patterns):

he	tree	there
we	three	where
	wee	

 Transfer Rhyming Patterns

- Have students use rhyming words to spell **be**, **bee**, **free**, **flee**, and **agree**.

Lesson 50
throughout

Homophones **threw** and **through** are included in this lesson and the preceding lesson.

Lesson Focus: Homophones: **our**, **hour**; **through**, **threw** (from previous lesson)

Letters: <u>o</u> <u>o</u> <u>u</u> <u>u</u> <u>g</u> <u>h</u> <u>h</u> <u>r</u> <u>t</u> <u>t</u>

 Make Words: got hot hut rut rug hug out our hour trot truth thought through throughout

Directions: Tell the children how many letters to use to make each word.

- Emphasize how changing just one letter or rearranging letters makes different words:

  "Add a letter to **our** to spell the **hour** that is 60 minutes."

  "Change 1 letter in **rut** to spell **rug**."

- When the children are not just adding or changing one letter, cue them to start over:

  "Start over and use 5 letters to spell **truth**."

- Give meaning or sentence clues when needed to clarify the word the students are making:

  "Use 7 letters to spell **through**. We walked home **through** the park."

- Give the children one minute to figure out the secret word and then give clues if needed:

  "Our secret word is a compound word combining two words you already made."

 Sort Homophones: **our**, **hour**; **through**, **threw** (from previous lesson)

- Give a sentence to make the meaning clear.

Sort Rhymes: (with same spelling patterns):

trot	rut	hug	out
hot	hut	rug	trout

 Transfer Rhyming Patterns

- Have students use rhyming words to spell **clout**, **pout**, **about**, **spout**, and **without**.

Lesson 51
mailboxes

Lesson Focus: spelling change: **es** is added when words end in **x**
homophones: **mail, male; sail, sale**

Letters: a e i o b l m s x

 Make Words: ax Max box mile male mail sail sale lame lime slime/smile blame boxes mailboxes

Directions: Tell the children how many letters to use to make each word.

- Emphasize how changing just one letter or rearranging letters makes different words:

   "Add a letter to **ax** to spell the name **Max**."

   "Change 1 letter in **mile** to spell **male**. A man or a boy is a **male**."

   "Use the same letters in **slime** to spell **smile**."

- When the children are not just adding or changing one letter, cue them to start over:

   "Start over and use 5 letters to spell **blame**."

- Give meaning or sentence clues when needed to clarify the word the students are making:

   "Use 4 letters to spell **lame**. When someone can't walk, we say he or she is **lame**."

- Give the children one minute to figure out the secret word and then give clues if needed:

   "Our secret word is related to the word **mail**."

 Sort Homophones: mail, male; sail, sale

- Give a sentence to make the meaning clear.

Sort Related Words: box, boxes; mail, mailboxes

- Use related words in a sentence that shows relationship.

Sort Rhymes: (with same spelling patterns):

ax	mail	sale	smile	lime	lame
Max	sail	male	mile	slime	blame

 Transfer Related Words

- Have students use related words to spell **foxes**, **mixes**, and **taxes**.

Transfer Rhyming Patterns

- Have students use rhyming words to spell **wax**, **relax**, **flame**, and **frame**.

Lesson 52

government

Lesson Focus: suffixes **er**, **ment**
spelling change: drop final **e** when adding **er**
prefix **re**, meaning back

Letters: | e | e | o | g | m | n | n | r | t | v |

 Make Words: rent   vent   vote/veto   move   ever   never/nerve   event   voter   mover
remove   remote   govern   government

Directions: Tell the children how many letters to use to make each word.

- Emphasize how changing just one letter or rearranging letters makes different words:

    "Change 1 letter in **rent** to spell **vent**."

    "Use the same letters in **vote** to spell **veto**."

    "Add a letter to **ever** to spell **never**. I would **never** do that."

- When the children are not just adding or changing one letter, cue them to start over:

    "Start over and use 5 letters to spell **event**."

- Give meaning or sentence clues when needed to clarify the word the students are making:

    "Use 6 letters to spell **govern**. When you mange or rule a place, you **govern** it."

- Give the children one minute to figure out the secret word and then give clues if needed:

    "Our secret word is related to the word **govern**."

 Sort Related Words: vote, voter; mover, mover, remove; govern, government

- Use related words in a sentence that shows relationship.

Sort Rhymes: (with same spelling patterns):

rent	ever	vote
vent	never	remote
event		

 Transfer Related Words

- Have students use related words to spell **payment**, **statement**, and **apartment**.

Transfer Rhyming Patterns

- Have students use rhyming words to spell **clever**, **note**, **quote**, and **wrote**.

62

Lesson 53
measurement

Lesson Focus: suffixes **ment**, **est**
prefix **re**, meaning again
homophones: **meat**, **meet**

Letters: | a | e | e | e | u | m | m | n | r | s | t |

 Make Words: set seat meat meet same name/mean near amuse rename
meanest nearest measure amusement measurement

Directions: Tell the children how many letters to use to make each word.

- Emphasize how changing just one letter or rearranging letters makes different words:

   "Add a letter to **set** to spell the **seat**. Sit in your **seat**."

   "Change 1 letter in **seat** to spell **meat**."

   "Use the same letters in **name** to spell **mean**. Don't be **mean**."

- When the children are not just adding or changing one letter, cue them to start over:

   "Start over and use 5 letters to spell **amuse**. What will **amuse** little children?"

- Give meaning or sentence clues when needed to clarify the word the students are making:

   "Use 7 letters to spell **measure**. The ruler will help us **measure** the length."

- Give the children one minute to figure out the secret word and then give clues if needed:

   "Our secret word is related to the word **measure**."

 Sort Homophones: meat, meet

- Give a sentence to make the meaning clear.

Sort Related Words: name, rename; mean, meanest; near, nearest;
amuse, amusement; measure, measurement

- Use related words in a sentence that shows relationship.

Sort Rhymes: (with same spelling patterns):

| seat | same |
| meat | name |

 Transfer Related Words

- Have students use related words to spell **treatment**, **pavement**, and **shipment**.

Transfer Rhyming Patterns

- Have students use rhyming words to spell **tame**, **flame**, **shame**, and **became**.

63

Lesson 54

dangerous

Lesson Focus: suffix **ous**
homophones: **rode**, **road**

Letters: a e o u d g n r s

 Make Words: sang sung rung sung rode road sour sound round ground around garden/danger dangerous

Directions: Tell the children how many letters to use to make each word.

- Emphasize how changing just one letter or rearranging letters makes different words:

    "Change 1 letter in **sang** to spell **sung**."

    "Add a letter to **round** to spell the word **ground** that you walk on."

    "Use the same letters in **garden** to spell **danger**."

- When the children are not just adding or changing one letter, cue them to start over:

    "Start over and use 4 letters to spell **sour**."

- Give meaning or sentence clues when needed to clarify the word the students are making:

    "Use 4 letters to spell **rode**. He **rode** the bus home from school yesterday."

- Give the children one minute to figure out the secret word and then give clues if needed:

    "Our secret word is related to the word **danger**."

 Sort Homophones: road, rode

- Give a sentence to make the meaning clear.

Sort Related Words: rang, rung; sang, sung; round, around; danger, dangerous

- Use related words in a sentence that shows relationship.

Sort Rhymes: (with same spelling patterns):

sang	sung	sound
rang	rung	round
		ground
		around

 Transfer Related Words

- Have students use related words to spell **ahead**, **apart**, and **across**.

Transfer Rhyming Patterns

- Have students use rhyming words to spell **hang**, **hung**, **rebound**, and **playground**.

Lesson 55
mountainous

Lesson Focus: suffix **ous**

Letters: | a | i | o | o | u | u | m | n | n | s | t |

 Make Words: tan sun stun moon soon union onion suntan nation notion
motion mountain unanimous mountainous

Directions: Tell the children how many letters to use to make each word.

- Emphasize how changing just one letter or rearranging letters makes different words:

    "Add a letter to **sun** to spell the word **stun** that means to shock."

    "Change 1 letter in **union** to spell **onion**."

    "Change 1 letter in nation to spell **notion**. I have no **notion** of what you mean."

- When the children are not just adding or changing one letter, cue them to start over:

    "Start over and use 8 letters to spell **mountain**."

- Give meaning or sentence clues when needed to clarify the word the students are making:

    "Use 9 letters to spell **unanimous**. The vote was **unanimous**; everyone wanted to do it."

- Give the children one minute to figure out the secret word and then give clues if needed:

    "Our secret word is related to the word **mountain**."

 Sort Related Words: sun, tan; suntan; mountain, mountainous

- Use related words in a sentence that shows relationship.

Sort Rhymes: (with same spelling patterns):

sun	**moon**
stun	**soon**

Transfer Related Words

- Have students use related words to spell **joyous**, **famous**, and **nervous**.

 ## Transfer Rhyming Patterns

- Have students use rhyming words to spell **spoon**, **cartoon**, **balloon**, and **afternoon**.

Lesson 56

personal

Lesson Focus: suffix **al**
homophones: **sore**, **soar**

Letters: a e o l n p r s

 Make Words: pole role rope rose/sore soar lane plane/panel slope parole
reason person personal

Directions: Tell the children how many letters to use to make each word.

- Emphasize how changing just one letter or rearranging letters makes different words:

   "Change 1 letter in **pole** to spell **role**. Will you have a **role** in the play?"

   "Use the same letters in **rose** to spell **sore**."

   "Add a letter to **lane** to spell the **plane** that you fly in."

- When the children are not just adding or changing one letter, cue them to start over:

   "Start over and use 5 letters to spell **slope**. He skied down the **slope**."

- Give meaning or sentence clues when needed to clarify the word the students are making:

   "Use 6 letters to spell **parole**. The prisoner was released from prison on **parole**."

- Give the children one minute to figure out the secret word and then give clues if needed:

   "Our secret word is related to the word **person**."

 Sort Homophones: sore, soar

- Give a sentence to make the meaning clear.

Sort Related Words: person, personal

- Use related words in a sentence that shows relationship.

Sort Rhymes: (with same spelling patterns):

pole	rope	lane
role	slope	plane

 Transfer Related Words

- Have students use related words to spell **national**, **arrival**, and **removal**.

Transfer Rhyming Patterns

- Have students use rhyming words to spell **scope**, **telescope**, **flagpole**, and **tadpole**.

Lesson 57

electrical

Lesson Focus: suffix **er**, meaning more
suffix **al**
prefix **re**, meaning back or again
spelling change: drop final **e** when adding **er**

Letters:

a	e	e	i	c	c	l	l	r	t

 Make Words: tie lie lit call tall rate late later relit retie recall taller
recital electric electrical

Directions: Tell the children how many letters to use to make each word.

- Emphasize how changing just one letter or rearranging letters makes different words:

    "Change 1 letter in **rate** to spell **late**.

    "Change 1 letter in **lie** to spell **lit**."

    "Add a letter to **late** to spell **later**."

- When the children are not just adding or changing one letter, cue them to start over:

    "Start over and use 5 letters to spell **relit**.

- Give meaning or sentence clues when needed to clarify the word the students are making:

    "Use 7 letters to spell **recital**. My piano **recital** is on Sunday.

- Give the children one minute to figure out the secret word and then give clues if needed:

    "Our secret word is related to the word **electric**."

Sort Related Words: tie, retie; lit, relit; call, recall; tall, taller; late, later;
electric, electrical

- Use related words in a sentence that shows relationship.

Sort Rhymes: (with same spelling patterns):

tie	**call**	**late**
lie	**tall**	**rate**

 Transfer Related Words

- Have students use related words to spell **magical**, **musical**, and **logical**.

Transfer Rhyming Patterns

- Have students use rhyming words to spell **rebate**, **debate**, **migrate**, and **inflate**.

Lesson 58
sensible

Lesson Focus: suffixes **en**, **ible**
homophones: **be**, **bee**

Letters: | e | e | i | b | l | n | s | s |

 Make Words: be bee eel/Lee see sees seen less bless bliss sense lessen sensible

Directions: Tell the children how many letters to use to make each word.

- Emphasize how changing just one letter or rearranging letters makes different words:

  "Add a letter to **be** to spell the **bee** that is an insect."

  "Use the same letters in **eel** to spell the name **Lee**."

  "Change 1 letter in **sees** to spell **seen**. Have you **seen** my pencil?"

- When the children are not just adding or changing one letter, cue them to start over:

  "Start over and use 4 letters to spell **less**."

- Give meaning or sentence clues when needed to clarify the word the students are making:

  "Add a letter to **less** to spell **bless**. The priest will **bless** the couple getting married."

- Give the children one minute to figure out the secret word and then give clues if needed:

  "Our secret word is related to the word **sense**."

Sort Homophones: be, bee

- Give a sentence to make the meaning clear.

Sort Related Words: see, sees, seen; less, lessen; sense, sensible

- Use related words in a sentence that shows relationship.

Sort Rhymes: (with same spelling patterns):

bee	less
see	bless
Lee	

Transfer Related Words

- Have students use related words to spell **tighten**, **shorten**, and **sharpen**.

Transfer Rhyming Patterns

- Have students use rhyming words to spell **chess**, **dress**, **mess**, and **stress**.

Lesson 59

impossible

Lesson Focus: prefix **im**, meaning opposite

Letters: | e | i | i | o | b | l | m | p | s | s |

 Make Words: oil boil soil miss mess moss boss loss less bless bliss spoil simple possible impossible

Directions: Tell the children how many letters to use to make each word.

- Emphasize how changing just one letter or rearranging letters makes different words:

  "Add a letter to **oil** to spell the **boil** that you do with water."

  "Change 1 letter in **boil** to spell **soil**."

  "Change one letter in **bless** to spell **bliss**, meaning happiness or great joy."

- When the children are not just adding or changing one letter, cue them to start over:

  "Start over and use 5 letters to spell **spoil**."

- Give meaning or sentence clues when needed to clarify the word the students are making:

  "Use 6 letters to spell **simple**. The answer was **simple**."

- Give the children one minute to figure out the secret word and then give clues if needed:

  "Our secret word is related to the word **possible**."

 Sort Related Words: possible, impossible

- Use related words in a sentence that shows relationship.

Sort Rhymes: (with same spelling patterns):

oil	mess	miss	moss
boil	less	bliss	boss
soil	bless		
spoil			

 Transfer Related Words

- Have students use related words to spell **imperfect**, **impatient**, and **immature**.

Transfer Rhyming Patterns

- Have students use rhyming words to spell **kiss**, **loss**, **cross**, and **across**.

Lesson 60
incomplete

Lesson Focus: suffix **tion**

prefix **in**, meaning opposite

Letters: | e e i o c l m n p t |

 Make Words: pie   pile   tile   mile/lime   time   lemon/melon   elect   police   compete   complete   election   policemen   incomplete

Directions: Tell the children how many letters to use to make each word.

- Emphasize how changing just one letter or rearranging letters makes different words:

    "Add a letter to **pie** to spell **pile**. On the desk was a **pile** of books."

    "Change 1 letter in **pile** to spell **tile**."

    "Use the same letters in **lemon** to spell **melon**."

- When the children are not just adding or changing one letter, cue them to start over:

    "Start over and use 5 letters to spell **elect**. I wonder who we will **elect** for the class president this year."

- Give meaning or sentence clues when needed to clarify the word the students are making:

    "Use 7 letters to spell **compete**. Will you **compete** in the track meet this year?"

- Give the children one minute to figure out the secret word and then give clues if needed:

    "Our secret word is related to the word **complete**."

 Sort Related Words: **elect, election; police, policemen; complete, incomplete**

- Use related words in a sentence that shows relationship.

Sort Rhymes: (with same spelling patterns):

pile	**time**	**compete**
tile	**lime**	**complete**
mile		**incomplete**

 Transfer Related Words

- Have students use related words to spell **insane**, **completion**, and **selection**.

Transfer Rhyming Patterns

- Have students use rhyming words to spell **slime**, **prime**, **crime**, and **lifetime**.

Lesson 61
weakness

Lesson Focus: suffixes **ness**, **en**
spelling change: drop final **e** when adding **en**
homophones: **see, sea; new, knew; weak, week**

Letters: | a | e | e | k | n | s | s | w |

 Make Words: see sea new knew knee week weak/wake snake/sneak
seesaw wakens weakens weakness

Directions: Tell the children how many letters to use to make each word.

- Emphasize how changing just one letter or rearranging letters makes different words:

  "Change 1 letter in **see** to spell the **sea** that we can swim in."

  "Add a letter to **new** to spell **knew**. He **knew** the answer."

  "Use the same letters in **weak** to spell **wake**."

- When the children are not just adding or changing one letter, cue them to start over:

  "Start over and use 5 letters to spell **snake**."

- Give meaning or sentence clues when needed to clarify the word the students are making:

  "Use 6 letters to spell **seesaw**. The little boy liked to ride up and down on the **seesaw**."

- Give the children one minute to figure out the secret word and then give clues if needed:

  "Our secret word is related to the word **weak**."

Sort Homophones: see, sea; new, knew; weak, week

- Give a sentence to make the meaning clear.

Sort Related Words: weak, weakens, weakness; wake, wakens

- Use related words in a sentence that shows relationship.

Sort Rhymes: (with same spelling patterns):

see	weak	wake
knee	sneak	snake

 Transfer Related Words

- Have students use related words to spell **harden**, **hardness**, and **softness**.

Transfer Rhyming Patterns

- Have students use rhyming words to spell **squeak**, **streak**, **quake**, and **earthquake**.

Lesson 62

unhappiness

Lesson Focus: suffix **ness**

spelling change: **es** is added when words end in **sh**

spelling change: change the **y** to **i** and add **ness**

prefix **un** meaning opposite

Letters: | a | e | i | u | h | n | n | p | p | s | s |

 Make Words: sun pin spin spun push pine spine shine unpin pushes punish punishes sunshine happiness unhappiness

Directions: Tell the children how many letters to use to make each word.

- Emphasize how changing just one letter or rearranging letters makes different words:

    "Add a letter to **pin** to spell **spin**."

    "Change 1 letter in **spin** to spell **spun**."

    "Add 2 letters to **punish** to spell **punishes**."

- When the children are not just adding or changing one letter, cue them to start over:

    "Start over and use 8 letters to spell **sunshine**."

- Give meaning or sentence clues when needed to clarify the word the students are making:

    "Use 6 letters to spell **punish**. Will your parents **punish** you for being late?"

- Give the children one minute to figure out the secret word and then give clues if needed:

    "Our secret word is related to the word **happy**."

 Sort Related Words: **pin, unpin; spin, spun; push, pushes; punish, punishes; sun, shine, sunshine; happiness, unhappiness**

- Use related words in a sentence that shows relationship. Ask students how to spell **happy** and remind them that **y** changes to **i** when many endings are added.

Sort Rhymes: (with same spelling patterns):

sun	**pin**	**pine**
spun	**spin**	**spine**
		shine
		sunshine

 Transfer Related Words

- Have students use related words to spell **bushes**, **unready**, and **readiness**.

Transfer Rhyming Patterns

- Have students use rhyming words to spell **airline**, **define**, **grapevine**, and **shoeshine**.

Lesson 63
unworkable

Lesson Focus: suffixes **en**, **able**
spelling change: drop final **e** when adding **en**
prefix **un** meaning opposite
homophones: **no, know; new, knew**

Letters: <u>a</u> <u>e</u> <u>o</u> <u>u</u> <u>b</u> <u>k</u> <u>l</u> <u>n</u> <u>r</u> <u>w</u>

 Make Words: no   new   knew   know   able   lake   wake   woke   woken
broke   broken   unable   unreal   workable   unworkable

Directions: Tell the children how many letters to use to make each word.

- Emphasize how changing just one letter or rearranging letters makes different words:

  "Add a letter to **new** to spell the other word **knew**. I **knew** all the answers."

  "Change 1 letter in **knew** to spell **know**. I **know** how to subtract."

  "Add a letter to **woke** to spell **woken**. She has just **woken** up."

- When the children are not just adding or changing one letter, cue them to start over:

  "Start over and use 6 letters to spell **unable**, meaning not able."

- Give meaning or sentence clues when needed to clarify the word the students are making:

  "Use 8 letters to spell **workable**. The crossword puzzle was very **workable** for third-graders."

- Give the children one minute to figure out the secret word and then give clues if needed:

  "Our secret word is related to the word **work**."

 Sort Homophones: no, know; new, knew

- Give a sentence to make the meaning clear.

Sort Related Words: **wake, woke, woken; broke, broken; able, unable;**
real, unreal; work, workable, unworkable

- Use related words in a sentence that shows relationship.

Sort Rhymes: (with same spelling patterns):

lake	woke	woken
wake	broke	broken

 Transfer Related Words

- Have students use related words to spell **unclear**, **breakable**, and **unbreakable**.

Transfer Rhyming Patterns

- Have students use rhyming words to spell **spoke**, **spoken**, **pancake**, and **snowflake**.

Lesson 64
appreciate

Lesson Focus: homophones: **piece**, **peace**

Letters: | a a e e i c p p r t |

 Make Words: ate ice rice race part apart trace price peace pierce pirate repeat recite create appreciate

Directions: Tell the children how many letters to use to make each word.

- Emphasize how changing just one letter or rearranging letters makes different words:

   "Add a letter to **ice** to spell **rice**."

   "Change 1 letter in **rice** to spell **race**."

   "Add a letter to **part** to spell **apart**."

- When the children are not just adding or changing one letter, cue them to start over:

   "Start over and use 5 letters to spell **trace**."

- Give meaning or sentence clues when needed to clarify the word the students are making:

   "Use 6 letters to spell **pierce**. To **pierce** is to penetrate or make a hole in something. Many people have **pierced** ears."

- Give the children one minute to figure out the secret word and then give clues if needed:

   "Our secret word means to value something."

 Sort Homophones: **piece**, **peace**

- Give a sentence to make the meaning clear.

Sort Related Words: **part**, **apart**

- Use related words in a sentence that shows relationship.

Sort Rhymes: (with same spelling patterns):

ice	race	create
rice	trace	appreciate
price		ate

 Transfer Related Words

- Have students use related words to spell **along**, **across**, and **aloud**.

Transfer Rhyming Patterns

- Have students use rhyming words to spell **twice**, **advice**, **space**, and **fireplace**.

Lesson 65

wheelbarrows

Lesson Focus: prefix **re** meaning again
homophones: **war**, **wore**; **sore**, **soar**; **wear**, **where**; **hole**, **whole**

Letters: | a e e o b h l r r s w w |

 Make Words: war wore sore soar wear sale hole whole wheel where whale
labor resale browser wheelbarrows

Directions: Tell the children how many letters to use to make each word.

- Emphasize how changing just one letter or rearranging letters makes different words:

"Change 1 letter in **wore** to spell **sore**. I have a **sore** foot."

"Add a letter to **hole** to spell the **whole** that means all of it."

- When the children are not just adding or changing one letter, cue them to start over:

"Start over and use 7 letters to spell **browser**. If you browse the Internet, you are a web **browser**."

- Give meaning or sentence clues when needed to clarify the word the students are making:

"Use 5 letters to spell **labor**. **Labor** is another word for work."

- Give the children one minute to figure out the secret word and then give clues if needed:

"Our secret word is related to the word **wheel** and usually has three wheels."

 Sort Homophones: war, wore; sore, soar; wear, where; hole, whole

- Give a sentence to make the meaning clear.

Sort Related Words: sale, resale; wheel, wheelbarrows

- Use related words in a sentence that shows relationship.

Sort Rhymes: (with same spelling patterns):

wore	sale
sore	resale
	whale

 Transfer Related Words

- Have students use related words to spell **refund**, **rebuilds**, and **replace**.

Transfer Rhyming Patterns

- Have students use rhyming words to spell **scale**, **score**, **store**, and **restore**.

Lesson 66
dishwasher

Lesson Focus: spelling change: **es** is added when words end in **sh**
homophones: **herd, heard**

Letters: | a e i d h h r s s w |

 Make Words: ear hear dish wish wash wise rise herd heard arise dishes wishes washes radishes dishwasher

Directions: Tell the children how many letters to use to make each word.

- Emphasize how changing just one letter or rearranging letters makes different words:

  "Add a letter to **ear** to spell the word **hear** that you do with your ear."

  "Change 1 letter in **dish** to spell **wish**."

  "Change just 1 letter in **wish** to spell **wash**."

- When the children are not just adding or changing one letter, cue them to start over:

  "Start over and use 4 letters to spell **wise**. She was quite old and very **wise**."

- Give meaning or sentence clues when needed to clarify the word the students are making:

  "Use 5 letters to spell **arise**. When did you **arise** this morning?"

- Give the children one minute to figure out the secret word and then give clues if needed:

  "Our secret word is related to the word **dish**."

 Sort Homophones: **herd, heard**

- Give a sentence to make the meaning clear.

Sort Related Words: hear, heard; rise, arise; wish, wishes;
dish, dishes, dishwasher, wash, washes

- Use related words in a sentence that shows relationship.

Sort Rhymes: (with same spelling patterns):

ear	dish	wise	dishes
hear	wish	rise	wishes
		arise	radishes

 Transfer Related Words

- Have students use related words to spell **awake**, **asleep**, and **across**.

Transfer Rhyming Patterns

- Have students use rhyming words to spell **year**, **spear**, **revise**, and **franchise**.

Lesson 67
vegetables

Lesson Focus: homophones: **be, bee; see, sea; beats, beets**

Letters: | a̲ | e̲ | e̲ | e̲ | b̲ | g̲ | l̲ | s̲ | t̲ | v̲ |

 Make Words: be bee see sea seat late gate least beast/beats beets table stable elevate vegetables

Directions: Tell the children how many letters to use to make each word.

- Emphasize how changing just one letter or rearranging letters makes different words:

  "Add a letter to **be** to spell the **bee** that is an insect."

  "Change 1 letter in **bee** to spell **see**. I can **see** the bee."

  "Use the same letters in **beast** to spell **beats**."

- When the children are not just adding or changing one letter, cue them to start over:

  "Start over and use 4 letters to spell **late**."

- Give meaning or sentence clues when needed to clarify the word the students are making:

  "Change 1 letter to spell **beets**. I like to eat **beets** but not everyone does."

- Give the children one minute to figure out the secret word and then give clues if needed:

  "Our secret word is foods such as carrots, beans, amd corn."

 Sort Homophones: be, bee; see, sea; beats, beets

- Give a sentence to make the meaning clear.

Sort Rhymes: (with same spelling patterns):

bee	gate	least	table
see	late	beast	stable
		east	

 Transfer Rhyming Patterns

- Have students use rhyming words to spell **able**, **cable**, **locate**, **feast**, and **vibrate**.

Lesson 68
rollerblade

Lesson Focus: homophones: **role, roll; road, rode; board, bored**

Letters: | a e e o b d l l r r |

 Make Words: all ear rear ball roll role robe rode road board bored blade dollar earlobe rollerblade

Directions: Tell the children how many letters to use to make each word.

- Emphasize how changing just one letter or rearranging letters makes different words:

  "Add a letter to **ear** to spell **rear**."

  "Change two letters in **ball** to spell **roll**. The car was out of gas but could **roll** down the hill."

  "Change 1 letter in **roll** to spell **role** as in the **role** you want to act in the play."

- When the children are not just adding or changing one letter, cue them to start over:

  "Start over and use 5 letters to spell **board**."

- Give meaning or sentence clues when needed to clarify the word the students are making:

  "Use 5 letters to spell the other word **bored**. When you get tired of doing something, you get **bored**."

- Give the children one minute to figure out the secret word and then give clues if needed:

  "Our secret word is related to the word **roll**."

 Sort Homophones: role, roll; road, rode; bored, board

- Give a sentence to make the meaning clear.

Sort Related Words: ear, earlobe; roll, blade, rollerblade

- Use related words in a sentence that shows relationship.

Sort Rhymes: (with same spelling patterns):

all	ear	robe
ball	rear	earlobe

 Transfer Related Words

- Have students use related words to spell **earring**, **eardrum**, and **rollerskate**.

Transfer Rhyming Patterns

- Have students use rhyming words to spell **globe**, **probe**, **clear**, and **year**.

Lesson 69

horseback

Lesson Focus: suffix **er**, meaning person or thing that does something
spelling change: drop final **e** when adding **er**
homophones: **break**, **brake**

Letters: | a | e | o | b | c | h | k | r | s |

Make Words: back hack bake baker/break/brake broke choke horse shack shake shaker backers hackers horseback

Directions: Tell the children how many letters to use to make each word.

- Emphasize how changing just one letter or rearranging letters makes different words:

    "Change 1 letter in **hack** to spell **back**."

    "Add a letter to **bake** to spell the **baker**. A person who bakes is a **baker**."

    "Use the same letters in **baker** to spell **break**. We won't take a **break** right now."

    "Use the same letters again to spell **brake**. You put on the **brake** at a stop sign."

- When the children are not just adding or changing one letter, cue them to start over:

    "Start over and use 5 letters to spell **shack**."

- Give meaning or sentence clues when needed to clarify the word the students are making:

    "Use 5 letters to spell **horse**. Did you ever ride a **horse?**"

- Give the children one minute to figure out the secret word and then give clues if needed:

    "Our secret word is a compound word combining two words we made."

Sort Homophones: break, brake

- Give a sentence to make the meaning clear.

Sort Related Words: bake, baker; shake, shaker; back, backers; hack, hackers; horse, back, horseback

- Use related words in a sentence that shows relationship.

Sort Rhymes: (with same spelling patterns):

broke	bake	baker	hack	backers
choke	shake	shaker	back	hackers
	brake		shack	

Transfer Related Words

- Have students use related words to spell **biker**, **hiker**, and **lockers**.

Transfer Rhyming Patterns

- Have students use rhyming words to spell **joke**, **stroke**, **crackers**, and **racetrack**.

Lesson 70

birdhouses

Lesson Focus: spelling change: **es** is added when words end in **sh**
homophones: **our**, **hour**

Letters:

e	i	o	u	b	d	h	r	s	s

 Make Words: our hour bird shed dish rush brush shred houses dishes
rushes rushed brushed brushes birdhouses

Directions: Tell the children how many letters to use to make each word.

- Emphasize how changing just one letter or rearranging letters makes different words:

  "Add a letter to **our** to spell the **hour** that you use when telling time."

  "Add a letter to **rush** and you can spell **brush**. Did you **brush** your hair?"

  "Change 1 letter in **rushes** to spell **rushed**. I **rushed** to school this morning."

- When the children are not just adding or changing one letter, cue them to start over:

  "Start over and use 4 letters to spell **bird**."

- Give meaning or sentence clues when needed to clarify the word the students are making:

  "Use 4 letters to spell **shed**. We found the lost cat in the **shed** out back."

- Give the children one minute to figure out the secret word and then give clues if needed:

  "Our secret word is a compound word combining two words we made."

 Sort Homophones: our, hour

- Give a sentence to make the meaning clear.

Sort Related Words: rush, rushes, rushed; brush, brushes, brushed;
dish, dishes; bird, house, birdhouses

- Use related words in a sentence that shows relationship.

Sort Rhymes: (with same spelling patterns):

shed	rush	rushes	rushed
shred	brush	brushes	brushed

 Transfer Related Words

- Have students use related words to spell **wishes**, **crashes**, and **doghouse**.

Transfer Rhyming Patterns

- Have students use rhyming words to spell **crush**, **crushes**, **crushed**, and **bunkbed**.

Reproducible Letter Strips

1. o i g h n p p s
   _ _ _ _ _ _ _ _

2. e i d p p r t
   _ _ _ _ _ _ _

3. u i b b c g n r s
   _ _ _ _ _ _ _ _ _

4. a e b c h n r s
   _ _ _ _ _ _ _ _

5. a e c h r s s
   _ _ _ _ _ _ _

6. e o h p p r s s
   _ _ _ _ _ _ _ _

7. a e e d g n r r s
   _ _ _ _ _ _ _ _ _

8. a e l n n p r s

9. e e i b g n n r s

10. e o o c c l l r s t

11. i o u c n r r s t t

12. e i o c d r r s t

13. a e d d m s t

14. e i b g h r s t t

15. e o g n r r s t

_ _o_ g_ _ _ _ _ _

16. a e e i d d g r s

_ _ _ _g_ _ _i_ _ _ _ s

17. e i o c d r s v y

_ _ _ _ _ _ _ _ _y_

18. u e i c r s t y

_ _ _ _ _r_ _ _ _y_

19. e i u f n n s t

_ _ _ _ _ _ _ _t_

20. a e i u h n p p r

_a_ _ _ _ _ _ _p_ _r_

21. e o o f g n r t t

_ _ _ _ _g_ _ _ _ _

22. e o c h l s t
___ ___ ___ ___ ___ ___ ___

23. e e i g h n r t v y
___ ___ ___ ___ ___ ___ ___ ___ ___ ___

24. a e e i l p n r s
___ ___ ___ ___ ___ ___ ___ ___ ___

25. a a e b f k r s t
___ ___ ___ ___ ___ ___ ___ ___ ___

26. o u c d l n t '
___ ___ ___ ___ ___ ___ ___ ___

27. o u d h l n s t '
___ ___ ___ ___ ___ ___ ___ ___

28. o u d l n t w '
___ ___ ___ ___ ___ ___ ___

29. o o u c d n n t w
   _ _ _ _ _ _ _ _ _

30. e o u f l p r w
   _ _ _ _ _ _ _ _

31. e o u d f l n r w
   _ _ _ _ _ _ _ _ _

32. a e u c f l l r y
   _ _ _ _ _ _ _ _ _

33. a e h k l n s s t
   _ _ _ _ _ _ _ _ _

34. a e e c l l r s s y
   _ _ _ _ _ _ _ _ _ _

35. a e e i g h p p r t w
   _ _ _ _ _ _ _ _ _ _ _

36. a a i o c n s t v

37. e i o o c c n n n s t

38. e e i o n p r s s x

39. e i u g n n r r t

40. e i i g n r r t w

41. e e o d g k l n w

42. e e u b b l r r y

43. a e e u c r r s t

‾ ‾ ‾ ‾ ‾ ‾ ‾ ‾ ‾

44. a e e u d p r r t

‾ ‾ ‾ ‾ ‾ ‾ ‾ ‾ ‾

45. a e e u l p r s

‾ ‾ ‾ ‾ ‾ ‾ ‾ ‾

46. a a e e b c c l p t

‾ ‾ ‾ ‾ ‾ ‾ ‾ ‾ ‾ ‾

47. e e i o c n p s t x

‾ ‾ ‾ ‾ ‾ ‾ ‾ ‾ ‾ ‾

48. a e e h r t v w

‾ ‾ ‾ ‾ ‾ ‾ ‾ ‾

49. e e h h r t w

‾ ‾ ‾ ‾ ‾ ‾ ‾

Lesson 50-56

50. o o u g h h r t t

51. a e i o b l m s x

52. e e o g m n n r t v

53. a e e e u m m n r s t

54. a e o u d g n r s

55. a i o o u u m n n s t

56. a e o l n p r s

57. a e e i c c l l r t
___ ___ ___ ___ ___ ___ ___ ___ ___ ___

58. e e i b l n s s
___ ___ ___ ___ ___ ___ ___ ___

59. e i i o b l m p s s
___ ___ ___ ___ ___ ___ ___ ___ ___ ___

60. e e i o c l m n p t
___ ___ ___ ___ ___ ___ ___ ___ ___ ___

61. a e e k n s s w
___ ___ ___ ___ ___ ___ ___ ___

62. a e i u h n n p p s s
___ ___ ___ ___ ___ ___ ___ ___ ___ ___ ___

63. a e o u b k l n r w

Lessons 64-70

64. a a e e i c p p r t

65. a e e o b h l r r s w w

66. a e i d h h r s s w

67. a e e e b g l s t v

68. a e e o b d l l l r r

69. a e o b c h k r s

70. e i o u b d h r s s

Reproducible Homophone Book Cover

son/sun

flour/flower

deer/dear

bee/be

Name _____

Teacher _____

School _____

Reproducible Homophone Index

1. accept   except
2. ad   add
3. ate   eight
4. be   be
5. bear   bare
6. beat   beet
7. berry   bury
8. board   bored
9. break   brake
10. by   buy
11. close   clothes
12. dear   deer
13. flour   flower
14. for   four
15. heard   herd
16. here   hear
17. hole   whole
18. in   inn
19. knew   new
20. know   no
21. mail   male
22. meat   meet
23. one   won
24. our   hour
25. pail   pale
26. pain   pane
27. pair   pear

28. peace   piece
29. plain   plane
30. rain   rein
31. rap   wrap
32. right   write
33. road   rode
34. roll   role
35. sail   sale
36. sea   see
37. sell   cell
38. sent   cent   scent
39. sight   site
40. son   sun
41. sore   soar
42. steak   stake
43. there   their
44. threw   through
45. tied   tide
46. to   too   two
47. wait   weight
48. war   wore
49. weather   whether
50. we   wee
51. week   weak
52. where   wear
53. wood   would

Reproducible Page for Two Homophones

Homophones: _____ _____

1. _____

2. _____

Reproducible Page for Three Homophones

Homophones: _____ _____ _____

1. _____

2. _____

3. _____